At Sylvan, we believe anyone can master math skills and develop a love of reading, and we are glad you have chosen our resources to help your children experience the joy of both subjects as they build crucial reasoning skills. We know that time spent reinforcing lessons learned in school will contribute to understanding and mastery.

Reading comprehension is the foundation of success in all aspects of third-grade academics. As a successful reader, you hold infinite possibilities in your hands, enabling you to learn about anything and everything. Similarly, success in math requires more than just memorizing basic facts and algorithms; it also requires children to make connections between the real world and math concepts in order to solve problems. Successful problem solvers will be ready for the challenges of mathematics as they advance to more complex topics and encounter new problems both in school and at home.

We use a research-based, step-by-step process in teaching both reading and math that includes thought-provoking reading selections, math problems, and activities. The learning process also relies on high standards and meaningful parental involvement. With success, students feel increasing confidence. With increasing confidence, students build even more success. It's a perfect cycle. That's why our Sylvan workbooks aren't like the others. We're laying out the roadmap for learning that is designed to lead your child to success in school.

Included with your purchase of this workbook is a coupon for a discount at a participating Sylvan center. We hope you will use this coupon to further your children's academic journeys. Let us partner with you to support the development of confident, well-prepared, independent learners.

The Sylvan Team

Sylvan Learning Center.
Unleash your child's potential here.

No matter how big or small the academic challenge, every child has the ability to learn. But sometimes children need help making it happen. Sylvan believes every child has the potential to do great things. And, we know better than anyone else how to tap into that academic potential so that a child's future really is full of possibilities. Sylvan Learning Center is the place where your child can build and master the learning skills needed to succeed and unlock the potential you know is there.

The proven, personalized approach of our in-center programs deliver unparalleled results that other supplemental education services simply can't match. Your child's achievements will be seen not only in test scores and report cards but outside the classroom as well. And when he starts achieving his full potential, everyone will know it. You will see a new level of confidence come through in everything he does and every interaction he has.

How can Sylvan's personalized in-center approach help your child unleash his potential?

• Starting with our exclusive Sylvan Skills Assessment®, we pinpoint your child's exact academic needs.

• Then we develop a customized learning plan designed to achieve your child's academic goals.

• Through our method of skill mastery, your child will not only learn and master every skill in his personalized plan, he will be truly motivated and inspired to achieve his full potential.

To get started, included with this Sylvan product purchase is $10 off our exclusive Sylvan Skills Assessment®. Simply use this coupon and contact your local Sylvan Learning Center to set up your appointment.

And to learn more about Sylvan and our innovative in-center programs, call 1-800-EDUCATE or visit www.educate.com. *With over 1,000 locations in North America, there is a Sylvan Learning Center near you!*

3rd Grade
Reading & Math
Workout

Published in the United States by Random House LLC, New York, and in Canada by Random House of Canada Limited, Toronto.

A Penguin Random House Company.

www.tutoring.sylvanlearning.com

Created by Smarterville Productions LLC
Producer & Editorial Direction: The Linguistic Edge
Producer: TJ Trochlil McGreevy
Writer: Amy Kraft
Cover and Interior Photos: Jonathan Pozniak
Cover and Interior Illustrations: Shawn Finley and Duendes del Sur
Layout and Art Direction: SunDried Penguin
Director of Product Development: Russell Ginns

First Edition

ISBN: 978-1-101-88190-3

Library of Congress Cataloging-in-Publication Data available upon request.

This book is available at special discounts for bulk purchases for sales promotions or premiums. For more information, write to Special Markets/Premium Sales, 1745 Broadway, MD 6-2, New York, New York 10019 or e-mail specialmarkets@randomhouse.com.

PRINTED IN CHINA

10 9 8 7 6 5 4 3 2 1

3rd Grade
Reading Comprehension
Success

Contents

Checking your answers is part of the learning.

Each section of this workbook begins with an easy-to-use Check It! strip.

1. Before beginning the activities, cut out the Check It! strip.

2. As you complete the activities on each page, check your answers.

3. If you find an error, you can correct it yourself.

When you *predict*, that means you're guessing what the book is about before you read it. Smart readers predict before they read. Use the cover of a book to figure out what the story will be about.

Ask yourself what kind of story you are about to read. Is it a romance, science fiction, comedy, or mystery? These categories are called *genres*.

FILL IN the blank next to each cover with the genre you think it is.

science fiction   action   romance   horror

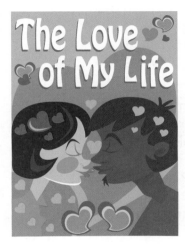

1. _____

2. _____

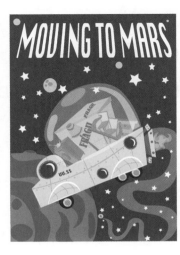

3. _____

4. _____

Pick the One!

CIRCLE the best title for each book cover.

1.

   a. The Old Man and the Sea

   b. The History of Baseball

   c. A Boy and His Dog

   d. School Stinks!

2.

   a. High School Dance

   b. The Popcorn Mystery

   c. Rocketship Down!

   d. Making the Team

3.

   a. Call Me Mister Pimple!

   b. Goldilocks and the Three Bears

   c. Kyle the Cowboy Kid

   d. Lost in the Mountains

4.

a. A Day in the Park

b. Summer Love

c. Going to Grandma's

d. Level Up!

5.

a. The Haunted House

b. Grounded for Life

c. Neighborhood Murder

d. Mrs. Frisby Moves Away

6.

a. Trapped with My Brother

b. I Hate Sisters!

c. Summer on Wheels

d. Ski Camp

Doodle Pad

CREATE a cover and title to match each plot.

Plot 1: Jeremy spends the summer with his grandma in a big house on Loony Lake. While he's there, he makes friends with Shania, the hot dog eating champion of Loony Lake. But at this year's hot dog eating contest, Jeremy is the winner! Will Shania still be his friend?

Title:

Plot 2: Starfire is a Native American girl. Johnny Kane is a young boy who's just joined the Pony Express to bring mail across the prairie. When Starfire saves Johnny from a robbery, they fall in love. Can two such different people find happiness?

Title:

Plot 3: In the mountain town of Belltoona, everyone's a pilot! The sky is filled with helicopters and mini-jets zipping through the air. Even the school bus has wings! But Chrissy Hepkins is afraid to fly. Will she face her fear or be the only kid in town riding a bike to school?

Title:

Plot 4: Twins Lucy and Andre are always fighting! Then one day, the twins are kidnapped by aliens from outer space. They have to get along and work together if they want to escape.

Title:

Predict & Confirm

Plot 5: Mayor MacBee's prized poodle has been dognapped. Everyone suspects crazy old Henry Hitchings. But Ricky "The Brain" Rodriguez isn't so sure. He's got to solve this mystery fast, before the wrong man goes to jail. The only problem: Ricky is in a wheelchair with two broken legs. Can he track down the missing poodle?

Title:

_____

Plot 6: When Arnold Jackson makes the Junior Pro Golf League, it's a dream come true. He's going to be the next Tiger Woods! But then, his mom gets sick—real sick. If Arnold drops out of the league to help take care of her, what happens to his dream?

Title:

_____

Check, Please!

CHECK the plot that's the best match to each cover.

1.

a. Thieves steal tons of gold bricks from Fort Knox.

b. A komodo dragon runs loose at a bake sale.

c. Gangsters steal the money from a church bake sale.

d. A little girl gets a new kitten.

2.

a. Jose's the best boarder on the hill until he's hurt in an accident.

b. Hillary and her brother fight over holiday candy.

c. Sanjay is accused of shoplifting, but it was really his friend Mike.

d. Maureen takes snowboarding lessons and becomes a champion.

3.

a. Candy Louis becomes a billionaire through babysitting.

b. A small town boy joins a famous rock band.

c. Missy Cooper lets her pop star fantasies get in the way of her real life.

d. A mother-daughter country music act travels all over the country.

Predict & Confirm

4.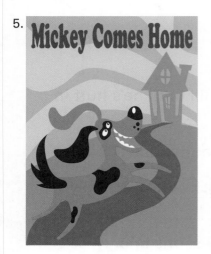

a. Betsy Johnson lost her cat and thinks her parents took it.

b. Isaac's parents want to know which one he likes better!

c. When Louisa's family plays Monopoly, the sparks fly!

d. Carlie's parents are getting divorced.

5.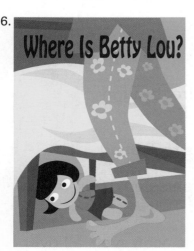

a. Mickey's little brother is a real pest, so he decides to run away.

b. When Mickey was little, he was terrible, but he grew up okay.

c. The Santos family loses their dog on vacation, but he finds his way home!

d. Mickey is king of the dog world and must fight a mean enemy.

6.

a. A little boy is kidnapped by spies.

b. Isa may be too old for dolls, but she has to find Betty Lou!

c. Betty Lou is stuffed with dollar bills.

d. There's been a murder in Dollville!

✓ Check It!

Cut out the Check It! section on page 1, and see if you got the answers right.

Now you know that when you read FICTION, you try to *predict* what the story is about before you start. When you read NONFICTION, think about what you already know about the topic. Here's an example:

Topic: Getting a Pet

FILL IN the blanks with things you know about this topic.

1. Kinds of Pets

cats

dogs

ferrets

_____

2. Pet Needs

brushing

visits to the vet

exercise

_____

3. Pet Stuff

toys

food dish

bed

_____

Check It!

FILL IN the blanks with things you know about each topic.

Topic: Helping the Planet

1. **You Can Recycle**

metal cans
_____
_____
_____
_____

2. **Don't Waste**

gasoline
_____
water
_____
_____

3. **Take Action**

pick up litter
_____
turn out the lights
_____
_____
_____

Topic: Summer

4. **Summer Vacation Places**
_____
_____
_____
_____

5. **Summer Clothes**
_____
_____
_____
_____

6. **Summer Activities**
_____
_____
_____
_____

7. **Summer Weather**
_____
_____
_____
_____

Skimming

When you SKIM an article, that means you don't read every word. Sometimes you might only read the *headings* (words in big, bold letters) and the picture captions. This is a good way to predict what you'll learn from the article! SKIM this article.

HINT: Notice anything funny about this page? We've already blurred the words you can skip.

Kids and Sports

The Most Popular Sports for Kids

Kids Love Sports Heroes!

Sports Are Good for Girls *and* Boys

The Bad Side of Sports: Injury and Competition

Sometimes sports can lead to injuries.

FILL IN the blanks with things you think you would read about in the article you skimmed.

Topic: Sports

1. **Popular Sports**

baseball

_____

_____

_____

2. **Famous Names in Sports**

Tiger Woods

_____

_____

_____

3. **Good Things about Sports**

Sporty kids make good leaders.

_____

_____

_____

4. **Bad Things about Sports**

Sporty kids might skip homework.

_____

_____

READ each statement about the article you skimmed. CIRCLE *True* or *False* for each statement based on what you learned from skimming.

1. It's never good for kids to play sports.   True   False

2. There are only three sports that kids can play.   True   False

3. Kids may be hurt while playing sports.   True   False

4. Sports are popular with kids.   True   False

5. Girls aren't very good at sports.   True   False

6. Kids don't care about sports heroes.   True   False

7. There's nothing bad about sports for kids.   True   False

8. Competition can sometimes go too far.   True   False

Skimming

SKIM this article.

100 Years of Movies

From Silent Pictures to 3-D: How the Movies Have Changed

Riusting ero euis auguer sed min ullaor sacte vent laoger cilit, consequ anconum ex euguerc illanet laoger cilit, consequ anconum ex euguerc illanet dio consectem doloreet num deliquat aut lummod te digna feum ex eu facum in et augian.

The Sky Is Filled with Stars: Movie Stars

Riusting ero euis auguer sed min ullaor sacte vent laoger cilit, consequ anconum ex euguerc illanet dio consectem doloreet num deliquat aut lummod dio consectem doloreet num deliquat aut lummod te digna feum ex eu facum in et augian.

In the early days, movies didn't have color.

A Century of Famous Films

Riusting ero euis auguer sed min ullaor Riusting ero euis auguer sed min ullaor sed min ullaor sed laoger cilit, consequ anconum ex euglaoger cilit, consequ anconum ex eugirconum ex euguerc dio consectem doloreet num deliquat audio consectem doloreet num, deliquat aunum deliquat aut lu te digna feum ex eu facum in et augiarte digna feum ex eu facum in et augiarcum in et augian.

Movies on the Move— You Can Watch Them Anywhere!

Riusting ero euis auguer sed Riusting ero euis auRiusting ero euis auguer sed min ullaor sacte vent laoger cilit, consequ anconulaoger cilit, conseqlaoger cilit, consequ anconum ex euguerc illanet dio consectem doloreet num dio consectem dolodio consectem doloreet num deliquat aut lummod te digna feum ex eu facum inte digna feum ex eu digna feum ex eu facum in et augian.

FILL IN the blanks with things you think you would read about in the article you skimmed.

Topic: Movies

1. **Changes in Movies Over 100 Years**

computerized special effects

2. **Famous Movie Stars**

George Clooney

3. **Famous Movies**

Star Wars

4. **Places You Can Watch Movies**

minivan

READ each statement about the article you skimmed. CIRCLE *True* or *False* for each statement, based on what you learned from skimming.

1. The movie business is failing.   True   False

2. Movies haven't changed much in 100 years.   True   False

3. There are lots of famous movie actors.   True   False

4. The first movies were in 3-D.   True   False

5. You can only watch movies in theaters.   True   False

6. Some movies have stayed famous for many years.   True   False

7. You can watch movies on an airplane.   True   False

8. Old movies didn't have color.   True   False

Check It!

Cut out the Check It! section on page 9, and see if you got the answers right.

Predict & Confirm

PICK a new story or book to read today. Before you start, FILL OUT this worksheet.

Predict

The name of the story is _____

I think the story will be about _____

_____

_____

_____

_____ .

Okay! Read your story, then fill in the next section.

Confirm

Was my prediction correct?   Yes   No

The story is about_____

_____

_____

_____

_____

_____ .

Predict & Confirm

PICK a new story or book to read today. Before you start, FILL OUT this worksheet.

Predict

The name of the story is_____

I think the story will be about _____

_____

_____

_____

_____.

Okay! Read your story, then fill in the next section.

Confirm

Was my prediction correct? Yes   No

The story is about_____

_____

_____

_____

_____

_____.

Reason to Read

PICK a new nonfiction story or book to read today. Before you start, FILL OUT this worksheet.

The title of my story is_____

Before you begin to read:

1. LOOK AT the book cover.

2. SKIM through the story.

3. ASK yourself what you know about the subject.

What do I know?

1. _____

2. _____

3. _____

4. _____

5. _____

Reason to Read

PICK a new nonfiction story or book to read today. Before you start, FILL OUT this worksheet.

The title of my story is_____

Before you begin to read:

1. LOOK AT the book cover.

2. SKIM through the story.

3. ASK yourself what you know about the subject.

What do I know?

1. _____

2. _____

3. _____

4. _____

5. _____

You already know how to predict what a story is going to be about. And you know to confirm your guess after you're done reading. What's left? REVISE. That's right! You revise your prediction while you read. Here's how it works:

1. What do you think this story is about?

_____

_____

_____

_____

READ this paragraph from the story.

> Ernie held onto the branch with all his strength. If his fingers slipped, he would slide down the cliff and fall a hundred feet! Suddenly he heard a familiar sniffing sound, followed by a whine. Carefully Ernie looked up to see Daisy Dawg, wagging her tail at the edge of the cliff.
>
> "Daisy!" cried Ernie. "Am I glad to see you!"

2. Now what do you think this story is about?

_____

_____

_____

If you changed your mind, then you REVISED your prediction. A good story will always keep you guessing.

Check It!

Page 21

1. The book could be about a boy who rescues a dog.
2. The story is about a dog that rescues a boy.

Page 22

1. The book might be about two kids who are being chased by a monster.
2. The book is about two kids whose identities and lives are erased, and they have to figure out why.

Page 23-24
Stop & Go Story

Did you choose Yes or No?

Page 25-26
Stop & Go Story

1. You might think Jake will use the money to buy a water gun.
2. You probably think Jake will use the money to buy a water gun.
3. You might think Jake will bring the money to the police.
4. You probably think Jake is going to use the reward to buy a water gun.

Check It!

Page 27-28

Stop & Go Story

1. Coach Krantz might be mad because something bad happened to him.
2. Coach Krantz might be mad because his team lost the game.
3. Coach Krantz might be mad because the waitress spilled his coffee.
4. Coach Krantz is mad because he broke his toe

LOOK at the cover. FILL IN the blanks with your prediction about the story.

1. What do you think this story is about?

_____

_____

_____

_____

READ this paragraph from the story.

> It was like they didn't exist and never had. Their teacher at school had never heard of a Jake or Letty Sitwell. For some reason, their parents didn't recognize them. Suddenly Jake smiled. They could do anything they wanted, right? Right!
>
> But Letty was way ahead of him. "There's the bus to the mall," she said. "I need a smoothie if I'm gonna figure out this mystery."

2. Now what do you think this story is about?

_____

_____

_____

Stop & Go Story

READ each paragraph. Then CIRCLE the answer to each question.

GO

In their secret hideout under Grizzly Mountain, the SuperSpy Team watched a message from their leader, X. "I've got bad news for you, SuperSpies," X said. "It looks like Doc Rotten has made a machine to change the weather. He's going to freeze Hawaii and melt the North Pole. We've got to stop him!"

The entire team jumped to their feet. "Let's go!"

STOP

Can the SuperSpies stop Doc Rotten?

Yes   No

GO

SuperSpy M and her kid brother Q zipped through the sky in their SpyShuttle. "I see him!" yelled Q, pointing. "Wow, that weather machine is *big*." They shot at Doc Rotten with their StingRays, but Doc Rotten sent a giant swarm of moths to knock their SpyShuttle out of the sky.

"You are now my prisoners!" shouted Doc Rotten.

STOP

Can the SuperSpies stop Doc Rotten?

Yes   No

GO

"I'll deal with you later," snapped Doc Rotten, leaving M and Q tied up. Then he started powering up his weather machine. It glowed with a red light. "Time to start some global warming!" the evil mastermind cackled.

"We've got to stop him!" cried M, tugging at the ropes. As they struggled, they heard a strange sound.

"Is that the weather machine?" asked Q.

STOP

Can the SuperSpies stop Doc Rotten?   Yes   No

GO

"It sounds like—like barking!"cried M.

It *was* barking! In fact, it was SuperSpy K9, running across Doc Rotten's evil lair. She used the laser beam on her collar to cut the ropes around M and Q, then she jumped at Doc Rotten, growling and showing her big teeth. M and Q turned off the weather machine just in time. When Doc Rotten was behind bars, the team called SuperSpy X. "We did it!" they shouted.

STOP

Did the SuperSpies stop Doc Rotten?   Yes   No

Stop & Go Story

READ each paragraph. Then FILL IN the blanks to answer each question.

GO

It's Jake's birthday, but he's miserable. His parents did *not* give him a 3XL Turbo-Shooter water gun like he asked for. Walking down the sidewalk, Jake kicks a lump of dirt. Wait! That's not a lump of dirt. It's a wallet! Jake picks it up and looks inside. It's filled with twenty-dollar bills!

STOP

1. What do you think Jake will do with the wallet?

_____

_____

GO

Jake counts the money quickly. There's enough to buy *ten* Turbo-Shooters! And the toy store is only a few blocks away.

STOP

2. What do you think Jake will do with the wallet?

_____

_____

GO

Just then Jake's pal Steffie zooms up on her scooter. "Hey Jake!" she says. "Whatcha got there?" When she sees the wallet, her eyes get big. "Whoa!" she says. "You better bring that wallet to the police. I bet someone's looking for it. That's a lot of money to lose."

STOP

3. What do you think Jake will do with the wallet?

_____

_____

GO

Steffie and Jake take the wallet to the police station. Standing at the counter is a big man with a very red face. He looks upset. When Jake puts the wallet on the counter, the big man pounces on it.

"My wallet!" he cries. "I'm so glad you found it!" He opens it up and counts the bills. "It's all there! Thank goodness." The big man pulls out sixty dollars and hands it to Jake. "Thank you for being honest, my boy."

Jake knows just what to do next.

STOP

4. What do you think Jake will do with the reward?

_____

_____

Stop & Go Story

READ each paragraph. Then FILL IN the blanks to answer each question.

GO

Coach Krantz was the nicest guy in town. But not today. Today the coach was *mad*. He yelled at the kids on the baseball team at morning practice. Then he snapped at the waitress in Joe's Diner at lunch. That afternoon he made a mean face when his neighbor waved at him and then slammed his front door.

STOP

1. Why do you think Coach Krantz is mad?

_____

_____

GO

The kids on Coach Krantz's baseball team were worried. "I bet Coach is mad at us because we lost the big game," said Jordan. The other kids nodded sadly.

STOP

2. Why do you think Coach Krantz is mad?

_____

_____

GO

Meanwhile, at the diner, Joe the cook found the waitress crying into her apron. "What's wrong?" he asked.

"Coach Krantz is mad at me," sniffled the waitress. "He's mad because I spilled his coffee at lunch today."

STOP

3. Why do you think Coach Krantz is mad?

_____

_____

GO

After Coach Krantz made a mean face and slammed the door, his neighbor, Mrs. Ling, was surprised to see a whole bunch of baseball players and a waitress walk up to his house. "What's going on?" she asked.

"We're here to say we're sorry," said one of the baseball players. "We all made Coach mad today."

Mrs. Ling rang the bell. When Coach opened the door, they saw that his foot was wrapped in a big bandage. "Coach, what's wrong with your foot?" asked Mrs. Ling.

"I broke my big toe when I tripped over my own shoes," said the Coach. "I'm so mad—it's been killing me all day!"

STOP

4. Why do you think Coach Krantz is mad?

_____

_____

 **Check It!**

Cut out the Check It! section on page 21, and see if you got the answers right.

The best way to remember all the great information you're reading is to stop every now and then. That will give you the chance to think about what you just read and make a list in your head, or notebook, of what you learned. Give it a try.

Stop & Go Story

GO

Growing Up Fast

How old does a doctor or a lawyer have to be? Not as old as you think. When Kathleen Holtz passed the California bar test to become a lawyer, she was only 18. That's right! She started college at 11, and entered law school at 15. And Balamurali Ambati became the world's youngest doctor at age 18.

STOP

1. What did you just learn?

_____

_____

GO

Other young professionals include film director Kishan Shrikanth (who made his first movie at age 10), cartoonist Alexa Kitchen (published at 7), and actress Anna Paquin (who won an Oscar when she was 11). Of course, when it comes to stuff like video games, kids rule! Victor De Leon III became a professional video gamer at age 9!

STOP

2. What did you just learn?

_____

_____

✓ Check It!

Page 29
Stop & Go Story

1. Someone became a lawyer at 18, started college at 11, and law school at 15. And the world's youngest doctor was 18.
2. There was a 10-year-old who directed a movie, a 7-year-old published cartoonist, an 11-year-old Oscar winner, and a 9-year-old professional video gamer.

Pages 30-31
Stop & Go Story

1. A roller coaster ride lasts about 2.5 minutes, the first big hill is called the "lift hill," and chains pull the cars up that hill.
2. Gravity and speed from the first hill can drive the roller coaster car for the rest of the ride.
3. Roller coaster cars can go as fast as 85 miles per hour on a steel structure. Wooden roller coasters only go as fast as 65 mph.
4. The brakes of most roller coasters aren't on the cars, they're on the tracks. The brakes are strong clamps that grab the car's wheels to slow them down.

Pages 32-33
Stop & Go Story

1. Some people get help from animals.
2. Seeing-eye dogs have been helping blind people for many years. Dogs can also tell by smell when a person needs medicine.
3. There are guide horses that help blind people who may be allergic to dogs. Horses also live longer than dogs.
4. There are helper monkeys that can open refrigerators and bring things to people who have to use a wheelchair.

Stop & Go Story

READ each paragraph. Then FILL IN the blanks to answer the question.

GO

A Wild Ride

A roller coaster ride may only last about 2.5 minutes, but there's a lot going on. At the start of the ride, your car needs to get up that first big hill, called the *lift hill*. Most of the time, there are chains pulling the cars up the lift hill (you can hear them clacking).

STOP

1. What did you learn about roller coaster rides?

_____

_____

GO

At the top of the lift hill, your coaster car lets go of the chains and gravity takes over. You slam through hills and turns and even loop-de-loops without any motors or electricity. Your car can run the whole ride using the speed it got from that first lift hill.

STOP

2. What did you learn about roller coaster rides?

_____

_____

GO

Roller coaster cars can go as fast as 85 miles per hour (over 135 kilometers per hour) if the entire ride is made of steel. But some roller coasters are made of wood. Wooden roller coasters can only go as fast as 65 mph (over 100 kilometers per hour). But they can *all* swish your stomach around!

STOP

3. What did you learn about roller coaster rides?

_____

_____

GO

Now it's time to hit the brakes. The brakes aren't usually on the cars, they're on the tracks. When the car comes to the end of the ride, strong clamps grab onto the wheels to slow them down. After braking, the car pulls into the station and the ride is over. Want to go again?

STOP

4. What did you learn about roller coaster rides?

_____

_____

Stop & Go Story

READ each paragraph. Then FILL IN the blanks to answer the question.

GO

Helper Animals

Some people need help because they're blind or in a wheelchair or sick. But who wants to depend on another human all the time? That's why we have helper animals. With a helper animal, you take care of the animal, and the animal takes care of you. That's only fair, right?

STOP

1. What did you learn about helper animals?

_____

_____

GO

Dogs have been helping blind people for many years. Seeing-eye dogs are specially trained to know how to cross busy streets and get through crowded sidewalks. Lately, scientists have learned that a dog's sense of smell is almost as good as a blood test. A dog can smell when some people are sick and can alert their human that it's time to take medicine. Pretty cool, huh?

STOP

2. What did you learn about helper animals?

_____

_____

GO

But dogs aren't the only helper animals. Some people are afraid of dogs or allergic to them. So there are also guide horses. That's right! Small breeds of horses, no taller than a grownup's hip, can also be trained to help a blind person get where they're going. Guide horses are better than dogs for people who don't want to keep their guide animal in the house. (Horses can live in a stable.) Plus, horses live a lot longer than dogs (40 years!), so you can train one to be with you for a long time.

STOP

3. What did you learn about helper animals?

_____

_____

GO

Neither dogs nor horses can open the refrigerator and bring a drink to a person in a wheelchair. So that's why there are also helper monkeys! Monkeys are really smart, and they have hands that can press buttons and carry things for people who can't. Monkeys, horses, and dogs help people every day. If you try, you can probably think of even more wonderful helper animals!

STOP

4. What did you learn about helper animals?

_____

_____

Stop & Go Story

READ each paragraph. Then FILL IN the blanks to answer the question.

GO

Arthur Ashe

When Arthur Ashe was five, his father got a really cool job. He was caretaker of a big park in Richmond, Virginia. The family moved to a house right in the park. So they had a playground, a pool, and a bunch of tennis courts in their own backyard. Arthur learned to play tennis when he was very young, during a time when African Americans like himself were not even allowed to play tennis in certain places.

STOP

1. What did you learn about Arthur Ashe?

_____

_____

GO

When Arthur was almost seven years old, a very sad thing happened. His mom died. He started to play tennis all the time, maybe because he missed her so much. But he also graduated at the top of his high school class and was the first member of the Ashe family to graduate from college.

STOP

2. What kind of *kid* was Arthur Ashe?

_____

_____

GO

All Arthur's tennis practice paid off. He became the first African-American man to be on the U.S. Davis Cup tennis team. He won the very first U.S. Open tennis tournament. And in 1975, Arthur Ashe was ranked the number one male tennis player in the whole world!

STOP

3. What did you learn about Arthur Ashe?

_____

_____

GO

But being a famous tennis player wasn't enough. While Arthur Ashe was growing up in Virginia, he saw black people treated differently than white people. That started to change as he got older. But in South Africa, it was still legal to treat black people badly. So Arthur became an activist—he spoke out against the government of South Africa. He went to South Africa as the first black professional tennis player, and the black South Africans called him "Sipho," which means "a gift from God."

STOP

4. What kind of *man* was Arthur Ashe?

_____

_____

Let's continue the story.

GO

> Then something terrible happened. Arthur had a heart attack! He had to stop playing tennis in 1980. A few years later, he needed an operation. At this time, people didn't know much about HIV or AIDS. Arthur got HIV from the blood they gave him during the operation. He talked to the press about his illness so that everyone would learn about HIV and AIDS, and he raised money to help find a cure.

STOP

5. What did you learn about Arthur Ashe?

_____

_____

GO

> Arthur Ashe died in February 1993. He was fifty years old. Almost 6,000 people attended his funeral in Richmond, Virginia, where they placed a statue of him on the town's famous Monument Avenue. Today, the main tennis court of the U.S. Open is called Arthur Ashe Stadium, after the first man (white or black) who won that tournament.

STOP

6. Why do you think so many people went to Arthur Ashe's funeral?

_____

_____

 **Check It!**

Cut out the Check It! to see if you got the answers right.

Predict & Revise

PICK a new fiction story or book to read today. As you read, FILL OUT this worksheet.

Predict

The name of the story is _____

I think the story will be about _____

_____

_____.

Okay! Read a little bit of your story, and then fill out the next box.

Revise

Do I want to change my prediction? Yes   No

Now I think _____

_____.

I think so because _____

_____

_____.

Now finish your story, and come back to fill out this box.

Confirm

Was my revised prediction correct? Yes   No

The story is about _____

_____

_____.

Predict & Revise

PICK a new fiction story or book to read today. As you read, FILL OUT this worksheet.

Predict

The name of the story is_____

I think the story will be about_____

_____

_____ .

Okay! Read a little bit of your story, and then fill out the next box.

Revise

Do I want to change my prediction?   Yes   No

Now I think_____

_____ .

I think so because_____

_____

_____ .

Now finish your story, and come back to fill out this box.

Confirm

Was my revised prediction correct?   Yes   No

The story is about_____

_____

_____ .

Keep Track of the Facts

PICK a new nonfiction story or book to read today. As you read, FILL OUT this worksheet.

As you're reading, STOP every so often and THINK about what you've read. Use this worksheet to keep track of what you're learning.

Part way through

What did I learn?_____

_____

What else did I learn?_____

_____

Halfway through

What did I learn?_____

_____

What else did I learn?_____

_____

Almost through

What did I learn?_____

_____

What else did I learn?_____

_____

Keep Track of the Facts

PICK a new nonfiction story or book to read today. As you read, FILL OUT this worksheet.

As you're reading, STOP every so often and THINK about what you've read. Use this worksheet to keep track of what you're learning.

Part way through

What did I learn?_____

_____

What else did I learn?_____

_____

Halfway through

What did I learn?_____

_____

What else did I learn?_____

_____

Almost through

What did I learn?_____

_____

What else did I learn?_____

_____

Reading is all about words, right? Wrong! While you read, you need to VISUALIZE. That means you make a picture in your head of what you're reading, like watching a movie!

READ each sentence, and CHECK the picture that matches it best.

1. Jack and Jill ran up the hill to fetch a pail of water.

a.

b.

c.

2. Jack fell down the hill and a dinosaur ate him.

a.

b.

c.

3. Jill grabbed her magic wand and turned the dinosaur into a butterfly.

a.

b.

c.

See how it works? Every good story makes a picture in your head.

4. Gerald lay in bed, watching the monster climb through his window.

a.

b.

c.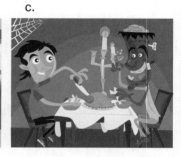

5. Marvin's father has a long black beard.

a.

b.

c.

6. Cindi woke up with a big, red pimple on her nose.

a.

b.

c.

7. Baby kangaroos sleep in a pouch on their mother's belly.

a.

b.

c.

8. Our house was brand new, with big windows and a blue front door.

a.

b.

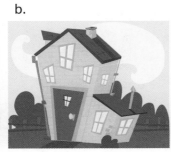

c.

9. Jimbo the Space Alien had bushy eyebrows, giant teeth, and a big smile.

a.

b.

c.

Doodle Pad

READ the paragraph and DRAW the picture it makes in your head.

Have you ever really looked at a fly? The common housefly can be up to half an inch long. Its wingspan is even longer! It has transparent wings, six jointed legs, and two giant red eyes on either side of its head. Behind the fly's head is its *thorax*, which is gray with four black stripes and shaped like a teardrop. Then comes its *abdomen*, which is a longer (kind of hairy) oval that ends in a stumpy little tail. Two tiny antennae stick out from between its eyes (where a human nose would be).

DRAW the common housefly here:

Doodle Pad

READ the paragraph and DRAW the picture it makes in your head.

> On the first day of camp, we met our counselor, Trixie. She had lots of freckles, and red hair that she always wore in two short braids. Her smile was big and friendly, but her braces were usually full of whatever she ate for lunch. For some reason, Trixie liked to wear wild clothes that were way too big for her. And get this: She was always doing yo-yo tricks. Seriously! She could do anything with her crazy yo-yo. But everyone in my cabin liked her right away. We just knew she was cool, even if she looked a little weird!

DRAW Trixie here:

Doodle Pad

READ the paragraph and DRAW the picture it makes in your head.

Zeke opened his eyes. He was alive! The bright sun made his head ache. He turned over and felt sand beneath his hands. He was on a beach! All around him were pieces of the shipwreck: broken boxes, planks of wood, some furniture. The ocean stretched out forever. Zeke was thirsty. A few feet away, he saw some people sitting under a row of palm trees. Maybe those people had some water. He started to crawl across the sand toward the trees.

DRAW Zeke's story here:

Doodle Pad

READ the paragraph and DRAW the picture it makes in your head.

Every year since 1967, the Canadian city of Nanaimo has had a 36-mile bathtub race! The people who race (called *tubbers*) have to make their boats out of bathtubs. Serious tubbers build specially made tubs that fit inside real racing boats. Other tubbers get silly, dressing like mermaids or using rope to tie an ordinary bathtub onto a floating platform. No matter who wins the race, everyone has fun when the water is filled with bathtubs!

DRAW the Nanaimo bathtub race here:

Doodle Pad

READ the paragraph and DRAW the picture it makes in your head.

Standing on the tower, high above the front gate, Jared watched a band of men attack his father's castle. They were shooting arrows from their long bows at the men guarding the gate. The arrows bounced off the guard's shields. Meanwhile, some of his father's soldiers were heating up a giant bucket of oil. When it was really hot, they would pour it down on the invaders. But look! A bunch of new men on horseback were coming to join the attack. Jared couldn't just watch any longer. He had to join the fight!

DRAW the battle at the castle here:

So you're reading this great story and *wham*! You hit a word you don't know. Do you give up and stop reading? No! You figure out what the word means from the CONTEXT—that means how the word is used. Check it out!

READ this paragraph:

> When I had walked a block from home, it began to rain—hard. I decided to go back and get my geziblet. Back on the street, I opened the geziblet over my head and hurried to the comic book store.

Did you catch the made-up word?

Context Questions:

1. Is a *geziblet* a noun (object), a verb (action), or an

   adjective (description)? _____

2. When do you need a *geziblet*? _____

3. What do you do with a *geziblet*? _____

4. What's the real word for *geziblet*? _____

See how you used CONTEXT clues to figure it out? If you can figure out a made-up word, you can figure out real words too!

✓ Check It!

Page 49

1. noun
2. when it's raining
3. keep the rain off
4. umbrella

Page 50

What's the Word?

1. verb
2. Percy
3. ask his parents for a dog
4. to pester or bug someone to do something

1. adjective
2. a hill or pit
3. so they can go fast
4. high, vertical, sudden, sharp

Pages 51-52

What's the Word?

1. b
2. a
3. c
4. a
5. get in the way, prevent, or block someone from doing something

Pages 53-54

What's the Word?

1. c
2. b
3. a
4. b
5. dull, inactive, or lazy

✓ Check It!

Pages 55-56

What's the Word?

1. a
2. c
3. b
4. a
5. a short sword with
   a curved blade

What's the Word?

READ each paragraph, and then FILL IN the blanks by answering the questions.

> Percy really wanted a dog. Every day, he asked his parents to let him get one. But his dad was allergic to dogs. There's no way his parents would ever say yes. But Percy asked anyway—every day! Finally, his mother lost her temper. "Percy," she said, "we are never getting a dog, no matter how much you badger us. So you might as well stop asking."

1. Is *badger* being used as a noun,

   verb, or adjective? _____

2. Who was doing the badgering? _____

3. What did Percy do every day? _____

4. What does the word *badger* mean here? _____

   _____

> There are lots of different kinds of skateboard parks. But whether they have wooden ramps that tower above the ground, or deep pool-like holes, all skate parks have to give skaters a steep hill or pit so they can get up enough speed to do tricks.

1. Is *steep* being used as a noun,

   verb, or adjective? _____

2. What does *steep* describe? _____

3. Why do skateboarders need something *steep*? _____

   _____

4. What does the word *steep* mean here? _____

   _____

What's the Word?

Before you read the story, answer this question: What do you think the word *hinder* means? (It's okay to guess!)

_____

Now READ this paragraph and see if you change your mind.

> Grasshoppers were everywhere! They squashed under our feet in our log cabin. Worst of all, they were eating every bit of grass on the prairie, including our crops! Ma and Pa and Bertie and I rushed out to try and stop them. Ma couldn't run as fast as us because her long skirts hindered her from running. They dragged on the ground and caught on the bushes. Finally, she tied her skirts around her waist, and ran along much faster. But it was too late. The crops were gone.

1. How is *hinder* being used here?

   a. It's a noun.

   b. It's a verb.

   c. It's an adjective.

2. What was hindering Ma?

   a. Her skirts

   b. The grasshoppers

   c. Bertie

READ each context question, and CHECK the correct answer.

3. What was Ma trying to do?

   a. Climb a tree

   b. Read a book

   c. Run fast

4. What were Ma's skirts doing?

   a. Dragging and slowing her down

   b. Pulling her along faster

   c. Lifting her off her feet

5. Now what do you think *hinder* means? _____

   _____

   _____

What's the Word?

What do you think the word *listless* means? (It's okay to guess!)

_____

_____

Now READ this paragraph and see if you change your mind.

> If you think your pet is sick, there are two things to check before calling the vet. Is your pet eating? If your pet leaves a lot of food in his bowl, that's a bad sign. Is your pet active? If your pet becomes listless and won't play or be friendly, that's also a sign of illness. Pets need a lot of sleep, but too much sleep can be a bad thing!

1. How is *listless* being used here?

   a. It's a noun.

   b. It's a verb.

   c. It's an adjective.

2. What does a listless pet *not* do?

   a. Hide under the bed

   b. Play or be friendly

   c. Sleep or dream

READ each context question, and CHECK the correct answer.

3. What does a listless pet do?

 a. Sleep a lot

 b. Eat a lot

 c. Play a lot

4. Is a listless pet hungry?

 a. Yes

 b. No

5. Now what do you think *listless* means? _____

_____

_____

What's the Word?

What do you think the word *cutlass* means? (It's okay to guess!)

_____

_____

Now READ this paragraph and see if you change your mind.

> Traveling with a princess is a pain. She rides in her fancy coach, with guards on horseback all around her. Guards like me get wet in the rain, and cold in the wind, while she stays snug and warm. In case of attack, each guard must carry a long sword as well as a shorter, curved cutlass. The long sword is good for fighting a battle on horseback. But if a guard loses his horse and needs to fight another man on the ground, the cutlass works better. Hopefully, we won't need either on this trip!

1. How is *cutlass* being used here?

   a. It's a noun.

   b. It's a verb.

   c. It's an adjective.

2. Who carries a *cutlass*?

   a. The princess

   b. The horses

   c. The guards

READ each context question, and CHECK the correct answer.

3. How is the *cutlass* described?

   a. Long and straight

   b. Short and curved

   c. Snug and warm

4. When do you use a *cutlass*?

   a. In battle

   b. When it's dark

   c. When it's cold out

5. Now what do you think *cutlass* means? _____

   _____

   _____

Picture This!

PICK a story or book that you've already read. Then FILL OUT this worksheet.

The title is _____

Here's a drawing of what the story looks like in my head.

Picture This!

PICK a story or book that you've already read. Then FILL OUT this worksheet.

The title is _____

Here's a drawing of what the story looks like in my head.

Context Clues

PICK a new story or book to read today. When you see a word you don't know, FILL OUT this worksheet.

The word is _____

The word is used as a   NOUN   VERB   ADJECTIVE   ADVERB
(circle one)

From the context, I think the word means: _____

_____

_____

Now, LOOK UP the word in the dictionary. WRITE DOWN the definition.

_____

_____

_____

_____

_____

_____

Context Clues

PICK a new story or book to read today. When you see a word you don't know, FILL OUT this worksheet.

The word is _____

The word is used as a   NOUN   VERB   ADJECTIVE   ADVERB

(circle one)

From the context, I think the word means: _____

_____

_____

Now, LOOK UP the word in the dictionary. WRITE DOWN the definition.

_____

_____

_____

_____

_____

_____

A good story is about a main character (like Cinderella) with a problem (her stepmother won't let her go to the ball). The fun part is how the character solves the problem (hello, Fairy Godmother!). If you start to get lost in a story, look for the problem! Check out this story!

Slippy the Snowkid

The boys on the block made a kid out of snow. They called him Slippy!

Slippy the Snowkid was really cool. He made the best ice forts.

One day it started to get hot. Oh no! Slippy was getting slushy.

The boys brought Slippy to the ice rink! Now Slippy could stay cool.

1. Who's the main character of the story? _____

2. What's the main character's problem? _____

_____

3. How is the problem solved? _____

_____

✓ Check It!

Page 61

What's the Problem?

1. Slippy the Snowkid
2. Slippy's melting.
3. Slippy's friends bring him to the ice rink.

Page 62

What's the Problem?

1. Tessa
2. Tessa wants to be a cowgirl, but she lives in the city.
3. She finds a camp for cowgirls.

Page 63

What's the Problem?

1. Donnell
2. He doesn't have a birthday gift for his mom.
3. He does everything she asks all day.

Page 64

What's the Problem?

1. Jack
2. He is supposed to get money for the cow, but he gets beans instead.
3. Jack plants the magic beans and climbs the beanstalk. At the top, he finds a bag of gold.

Problem & Solution

✓ **Check It!**

Page 65

What's the Problem?

1. Olive
2. She wants to dress like a fairy for the picnic, but her mother says she'll be too cold.
3. She creates a "Fairy Firefighter" costume that's warmer than a regular fairy costume. And she wins a prize!

Page 66

What's the Problem?

1. Micah
2. His friend's shoplifting ruins his favorite day.
3. He decides to drop his friend and make a new one.

Page 67

What's the Problem?

1. The SuperSpies M, Q, and K9
2. They need to stop Doc Rotten and his gang from robbing the banks, but the robbers are invisible.
3. SuperSpy Q and Superspy M throw paint on the robbers so they can see them and capture them.

Page 68

What's the Problem?

1. Sanjay
2. Sanjay's two best friends don't get along.
3. Sanjay loses his pet rabbit.
4. Sanjay calls his friends and asks them to get along just while they're hunting for Attila. After that, they find out that being friends is easy!

What's the Problem?

Cowgirl in the City

Tessa wants to be a cowgirl. But she lives in the big city!

She lassos her teddy bear and puts a saddle on a chair.

Finally, the answer!

Cowgirl Tessa on the ranch!

1. Who's the main character of the story? _____

2. What's the main character's problem? _____

_____

3. How is the problem solved? _____

_____

_____

What's the Problem?

The Birthday Bind

Donnell woke up with a gasp. He completely forgot it was Mom's birthday!

He tiptoed out of the house before breakfast. He needed a gift, *fast*!

Donnell didn't have money for candy or a card or flowers.

So Donnell gave Mom a special gift. He did everything she asked all day. She loved it!

1. Who's the main character of the story? _____

2. What's the main character's problem? _____

_____

3. How is the problem solved? _____

_____

_____

What's the Problem?

Jack and the Beanstalk

Jack's mother sent him out to sell their cow. "Make sure you get lots of money for it!" she said.

But Jack didn't get money. Instead, he traded the cow for some magic beans.

"We need *money*, not magic beans!" his mother yelled. She pulled Jack's ear and sent him outside without any supper.

Jack decided to plant the beans. Maybe they were magic, maybe not. But something should grow, right? Then he slept outside because he knew his mother was still mad.

When he woke up, Jack was high above the ground! He was lying on a giant leaf that came out of a giant stalk. It was a beanstalk!

Jack climbed up the beanstalk, just to see how high it went. At the top, he found a magic land in the clouds. He also found a big bag of gold coins!

"Hey mom!" Jack said, coming back into the house. "Here's that money you needed." And he dumped the bag of coins on the floor.

That's the last time Jack's mother ever pulled his ear!

1. Main character: _____

2. Problem: _____

_____

3. Solution: _____

_____

_____

_____

What's the Problem?

HINT: Sometimes the problem can be a decision that the main character has to make.

Olive's town was having a big dress-up picnic. She wanted to wear her fairy costume, but her mother said no. "The party's outside and it's too cold," she said.

"I'll wear tights," Olive said. "And a cape over my sparkly pink tank top."

"Pants," said her mother. "Pants and a sweater."

"Fairies don't wear sweaters and pants!" yelled Olive.

"So be a firefighter," said her mother. "Firefighter are warmer than fairies."

Olive stomped up to her room. Her fairy wings were hanging in her closet next to her firefighter outfit. "Hmmmmm," she said.

At the party, they gave a prize to the best costume. "This year's winner is Olive!" said the man in charge. "The Firefighter Fairy!"

Everybody clapped. Olive was wearing fairy wings over her firefighter's jacket, and a crown instead of a helmet. Her firefighter boots were painted with sparkly pink paint.

"How does a fairy fight fires?" asked Missy, who was mean.

Olive rolled her eyes. "Duh!" she said. "I use my magic wand!"

1. Main character: _____

2. Problem: _____

_____

3. Solution: _____

_____

_____

What's the Problem?

Super Saturday

Every Saturday, Micah bought candy and comics and then hit the big skate park. It was his favorite day. One week he thought it would be cool if his friend Tony joined him. Wrong!

See, Tony took some candy, but he didn't pay for it. Then he put two comics in his bag and walked out of the store. When they got to the skate park, Tony was all smiles, but Micah felt sick.

"What's the matter?" asked Tony. "Want some candy?"

"You stole that candy," said Micah, "and some comics."

"Yeah, so?" Tony frowned. "Are you gonna tell on me? Are you a tattletale?"

Micah didn't know what to say. His Saturday was ruined.

The next Saturday, Micah grabbed his skateboard and rolled down the street. When he saw Tony at the corner, he flew straight past him. He bought his candy and comics like usual. When he got to the skate park, Tony was there. But Micah ignored him. He wasn't going to let some dishonest kid ruin his Saturday again. Sheila was skating at the park too, and she was really cool. Maybe she could be Micah's new Saturday friend.

1. Main character: _____

2. Problem: _____

_____

3. Solution: _____

_____

_____

_____

What's the Problem?

HINT: Sometimes the problem can be a decision that the main character has to make.

Doc Rotten Strikes Again

Back at Grizzly Mountain, SuperSpy X was giving his team another mission. "Doc Rotten has made an Invisible Ray. He's going to sneak into the Big Swiss Bank and steal all the money."

So SuperSpy Q, his big sister M, and their dog K9 flew to the Big Swiss Bank. They saw big bags of money floating out the front door!

"It's Doc Rotten and his evil gang!" cried M. "They're all invisible!"

How do you stop robbers you can't see? When the SuperSpies tried to shoot them with their StingRays, they missed. Even K9's superdog nose was confused.

"Ha ha ha!" laughed Doc Rotten. "You'll never catch us."

Then Q had an idea. He ran down the street and bought two cans of black paint from the hardware store. "Come on, Sis!" he cried, handing a can to M. "Throw paint toward the money bags."

When the paint landed on the criminals, the SuperSpies could see them. K9 growled, backing them into a corner, while M and Q wrapped them in SpyNets.

Q called X on his wrist phone. "We caught Doc Rotten," he said. "Mission accomplished!"

1. Main character: _____

2. Problem: _____

_____

3. Solution: _____

_____

_____

What's the Problem?

HINT: You can have more than one problem in a story too.

Rabbit Hunt

Sanjay had two best friends, Marcus and Cherryl.
Too bad they hated each other. Sanjay could never hang out with both of his best buds at the same time.

One day on the way to the vet's office, Sanjay's rabbit, Attila, got out of her carrier and hopped away. Sanjay couldn't find her anywhere!

He needed help. But which friend should he call? Cherryl lived the closest, but Marcus had sharp eyes. Sanjay decided to call them both.

"Okay" he said to them, "please try not to fight while we look for Attila."

Marcus and Cherryl frowned at each other. "Okay," they said grumpily.

They searched for a few hours. Marcus used his great eyesight, and Cherryl told him where to look. Finally they found Attila hiding under a bush in the park.

Sanjay was so happy, he took everybody to Pizza Heaven for a great time!

After that day, Marcus and Cherryl stopped hating each other. They found out that being friends is easy when you do it in threes!

1. Main character: _____

2. Problem 1: _____

_____

3. Problem 2: _____

_____

4. Solution: _____

_____

_____

When you're reading information, keep your eye on the main idea. A good nonfiction article or book should always present one main idea and give you a bunch of details about it. As you read, make sure you sort the details under the main idea.

Try it out! SORT these details under the right main idea. FILL IN the blanks with the details.

hooves	cleats	goalie	notes	mane
penalty	tempo	gallop	instruments	

1. Soccer

_____

_____

_____

2. Music

_____

_____

_____

3. Horses

_____

_____

_____

When you stop and think about what you're reading, remember the main idea, and sort those details!

READ the paragraph, and FILL IN the main idea and details.

HINT: The details are highlighted.

Crazy Collections

When you think of collections, you probably think about things like trading cards, rocks, or stamps, right? But some people have really whacky collections. Did you know there's a man in Germany with 2,500 mousetraps? How about a woman in Las Vegas who's collected 30,000 refrigerator magnets? There's even a town in Canada with more than 10,000 town signs from all over the world. And the largest collection of potato chip bags belongs to a man in Germany. Then there's the guy in Australia who's been collecting his own belly button lint since 1984! Now that's crazy!

What's the main idea? Crazy collections _____

List the details:

1. _____

2. _____

3. _____

4. _____

5. _____

READ the paragraph, and FILL IN the main idea and details.

Around the World in 194 days!

There are lots of ways to travel around the world. How much time do you have? In 1999, the first nonstop hot air balloon trip around the world took 19 days, 21 hours, and 55 minutes. Is that too fast for you? Then hop in a sailboat! It'll take you about 60 days to sail around the globe. Still too fast? Try a bike! It took Mark Beaumont 194 days to bike around the world. He rode about 100 miles each day, flew across the oceans, and camped or stayed in hotels at night. If you need to get around the world in a hurry, a nonstop airplane flight around the world only takes about 67 hours. Or hop on a satellite for an even quicker trip. Depending on how high up it flies, a satellite can orbit around the planet in about 100 minutes! Let's go!

What's the main idea? _Ways to travel around the world_____

List the details:

1. _____

2. _____

3. _____

4. _____

5. _____

READ the paragraph, and FILL IN the main idea and details.

Fast Foods

If you're feeling hungry, check out an extreme eating contest. It's more than just pies and hot dogs. At the World Lobster-Eating Championship, someone munched 44 lobsters in 12 minutes! In Nevada, a man ate 247 pickled jalapeño peppers in 8 minutes. Famous hot dog eater Joey Chestnut can also eat 182 chicken wings in 30 minutes (hold the celery!). Other extreme eaters suck down pancakes, matzo balls, shrimp, and pizza. Of course, watching these people stuff their faces might make you lose your appetite!

What's the main idea? _____

_____

List the details:

1. _____

2. _____

3. _____

4. _____

5. _____

6. _____

7. _____

8. _____

9. _____

READ the story, and FILL IN the main idea and details.

HINT: Sometimes there are two main ideas!

Let the X Games Begin!

The X Games is the Olympics of extreme sports. It was started in 1995 by sports channel ESPN. Back then it was called "The Extreme Games." The name was changed to "The X Games" in 1996, and it stuck. Like the Olympics, there's a Winter X Games and a Summer X Games.

The X Games was created to cover sports that are not part of the Olympics. But one of its winter sports, snowboarding, was added to the Olympic list in 1998. And, of course, both events have skiing. But the X Games has an event called "Superpipe Ski" where skiers zoom through a half-pipe of snow, jumping and doing tricks like skateboarders. The Olympics hasn't added that (yet!). And the Olympics doesn't cover snowmobiling, another Winter X Games event.

The Summer X Games are even more different. In the summer, athletes compete in skateboarding, BMX bike races, motocross, surfing, and rallying (a kind of car racing). Compare that to Olympic events like gymnastics, softball, and table tennis!

Both the Olympics and the X Games have lots of fans. But X Games fans are younger, and as they grow in numbers, the Olympics will probably add more extreme sports to its line-up.

Now, TURN the page and FILL IN the blanks!

FILL IN the blanks with main ideas and details.

Main Idea 1: ___Winter X Games events___   Main Idea 2: ___Summer X Games events___

Details:

1. _____

2. _____

3. _____

Details:

1. _____

2. _____

3. _____

4. _____

5. _____

READ the story, and FILL IN the main idea and details.

Good Guys and Bad Guys

In the Old West, there were good guys and bad guys.

One bad guy, Billy the Kid, was a cattle "rustler" who stole cows and other livestock from people's farms. As for Black Bart, he used to rob the Wells Fargo stagecoaches that brought mail, money, and goods from the east. Black Bart robbed 28 stagecoaches!

On the good side, sheriffs like Seth Bullock kept law and order in wild western towns. And men like Charlie Parks worked hard to protect the mail. Parks started out as a rider on the Pony Express and then became a guard for Wells Fargo. Legend has it that he had more bullet wounds in his body than any other man in California!

Sometimes outlaw gangs would ride into towns and rob the banks. Butch Cassidy had "The Wild Bunch" gang. Jesse James had a gang called "The James-Younger Gang."

But there were good gangs too. The Dodge City Peace Commission, headed by famous sheriff Wyatt Earp, protected the people of their town. And the Pinkerton Agency sent detectives out west to hunt down outlaws like Jesse James and Butch Cassidy.

In the end, the good guys won out. Today people who live in the west know that their homes, towns, and mail are safe and secure!

Now, TURN the page and FILL IN the blanks!

Main Idea & Details

HINT: Sometimes there are two main ideas!

Main Idea 1: _____

_____

Details:

1. _____

2. _____

3. _____

4. _____

5. _____

Main Idea 2: _____

_____

Details:

1. _____

2. _____

3. _____

4. _____

5. _____

6. _____

Problem & Solution

PICK a story or book that you've already read. Then FILL OUT this worksheet.

Problem

The name of the story is_____

_____.

The main character wants_____

_____

_____.

The trouble that faces the main character is_____

_____

_____.

Solution

The way the character handles the trouble is_____

_____

_____.

The big idea of the story is_____

_____

_____.

Problem & Solution

PICK a story or book that you've already read. Then FILL OUT this worksheet.

Problem

The name of the story is_____
_____.

The main character wants_____

_____

_____.

The trouble that faces the main character is_____

_____

_____.

Solution

The way the character handles the trouble is_____

_____

_____.

The big idea of the story is_____

_____

_____.

Main Idea & Details

PICK a new nonfiction article or book to read today. As you read, LOOK FOR the main ideas and details, and WRITE them on this sheet.

My reading assignment is _____

Main Ideas	Details

Main Idea & Details

PICK a new nonfiction article or book to read today. As you read, LOOK FOR the main ideas and details, and WRITE them on this sheet.

My reading assignment is _____

Main Ideas	Details

You've read lots of stories, so you know how they work. A story is a bunch of events that happen in a certain order. If you keep track of these events, you'll know where you are in the story. Let's read one and see.

The Three Big Pigs

Hammy, Jammy, and Sammy were three big pigs. Hammy made his house out of straw. Jammy built his out of sticks. And Sammy constructed a big mansion out of bricks. One day, Wolfie Growl came to town. He liked to eat big pigs, so he went to Hammy's house. He huffed and puffed and blew Hammy's lame straw house down. Then he did the same thing to Jammy's house. But when Wolfie got to Sammy's big mansion, he blew until he was blue, but nothing happened. So Wolfie picked the lock, broke into the house, and ate up all three pigs. Burp!

Now, DRAW a line to match each event with its order in the story.

Order

1. First

2. Second

3. Third

4. Finally

Event

a. Hammy, Jammy, and Sammy build their houses.

b. Wolfie breaks into Sammy's house and eats all three pigs.

c. Wolfie can't blow down Sammy's house.

d. Wolfie Growl blows down Hammy and Jammy's house.

Easy, right? But sometimes the author doesn't tell you the story in the right order. So watch out!

 **Check It!**

Page 87

3
4
1
6
5
2

Page 88

3
1
4
6
5
2

READ the story.

Rain Delay

The Wildcats were winning. Their grand slam homerun in the first inning scored them four points. Then the Kingfishers got three runs in the second inning.

But it was so *hot*! By the sixth inning, sweat was streaming off all the Kingfishers in the outfield. The air was so thick, it was hard to breathe.

Suddenly, a little boy in the stands started to dance. He was Andy Kolchak's little brother.

"Stop!" yelled Andy, waving from the outfield. "*Stop*!"

But it was too late. Rain poured from the sky. The coaches ended the game early.

Andy took off his cap and smacked his brother in the behind. "Couldn't you have waited for us to tie the score before doing your stupid rain dance?"

"I was hot!" yelled his brother, dancing in the rain.

Now, DRAW a line to match each event with its order in the story.

Order	Event
1. First	a. The Kingfishers get three runs in the second inning.
2. Second	b. The game ends early and the Wildcats win.
3. Third	c. The Wildcats score four runs with a grand slam.
4. Finally	d. Andy's little brother does a rain dance.

READ the story.

HINT: Sometimes the author doesn't tell you the story in the right order. So watch out!

What's Justin's Problem?

After the big math test, Justin didn't know what to do. He felt terrible. Maybe he could talk to Mom? But when he went home, she had left for work. Justin lay on his bed. This is a serious problem, he thought.

At the bus stop the next day, Justin walked right up to his best friend, Mack.

"I saw you cheat on the math test yesterday," he said.

Mack looked sick and scared. "Are you going to tell Mr. Sam?" he asked.

Justin shrugged. "I don't know what to do."

The two boys didn't talk on the ride to school. Justin followed Mack off the bus and up the steps. At the doors, Mack turned around.

"Will you come with me?" he asked. "To tell?"

Justin smiled and said, "Of course! That's what best friends are for."

Now, DRAW a line to match each event with its order in the story.

Order	Event
1. First	a. Justin goes home and thinks about what to do.
2. Second	b. Justin tells Mack what he saw.
3. Third	c. Justin sees Mack cheat on the math test.
4. Finally	d. Mack and Justin go to tell the teacher.

Story Plan

READ the story.

Princess Pretty and the Beast

Once upon a time, there was a very ugly prince with a big scaly wart on the end of his nose. This prince also had hairy hands, hairy feet, and a hairy back. He even had sprouts of hair coming out of his ears!

The prince was named Zigfried, but everyone called him "Beast." He walked around looking at the ground and never smiled.

One day there was a carriage crash outside the prince's castle. The servants brought in a young lady who had hurt her head. The doctor said she needed to rest at the castle for two weeks with a cloth wrapped around her eyes.

Those two weeks were the best time Beast had ever had. The young lady was named Princess Pretty. She and Beast spent every day together, talking and laughing.

On the day the doctor returned, Beast ran away to hide. He was afraid that the princess wouldn't like him anymore once she could see.

When the doctor took off the cloth, the princess could see perfectly. She was so happy, she ran all over the castle to tell Beast. She found him in a very dark room.

"Hey Ziggy!" (She called him Ziggy.) "Are you hiding from me?"

"Um, no." Ziggy stepped forward into the light.

"Oh, dear!" the princess cried. "You really need a shave. And something must be done about that awful wart. Tsk-tsk-tsk!"

So Princess Pretty dragged the Beast to the nearest salon and had the barbers pluck his ears and wax his hands and feet. They trimmed his eyebrows and shaved his beard. They even took off his wart! When they were done, the princess gave Beast a kiss.

It worked like magic. Suddenly, Prince Ziggy stood up straight and smiled. He was really very handsome!

Now, DRAW a line to match each event with its order in the story.

HINT: Some of the events didn't happen in the story. Cross those out.

Order

1. First
2. Second
3. Third
4. Fourth
5. Fifth
6. Finally

Event

a. Princess Pretty breaks the fairy's spell.

b. Ziggy smiles and looks handsome.

c. Princess Pretty and Ziggy become friends.

d. The doctor takes off Princess Pretty's bandage.

e. Ziggy kidnaps the Princess from her home.

f. Princess Pretty ran away from the castle.

g. There's a carriage crash outside the castle.

h. An ugly Prince Zigfried never smiled.

i. Princess Pretty takes Ziggy to the salon.

Story Plan

K9 Saves the Day

One day, the SuperSpies were called to a meeting at Grizzly Mountain. Instead of seeing SuperSpy X, they saw a new SuperSpy, who wore a blue mask. He said his code name was D.

"Where's X?" asked SuperSpy Q.

"He's on a secret mission," said SuperSpy D. "So I'm in charge. And I have a special job for SuperSpies M and K9. We need to fly to Paris right away!"

So M and K9 left with SuperSpy D.

"That's weird," said Q. "I usually work with M and K9."

"Maybe the new guy doesn't know you're M's little brother," said SuperSpy T.

"Yeah, maybe you'll get your own missions from now on!" said SuperSpy F.

But Q was worried. He went for a walk around the underground SpyStation. He was passing a closet when he heard a strange knocking sound. He tried to open the door, but it was locked.

"SuperSpies T and F, I need your help!" Q called into his wrist radio.

T and F came running, and together the three spies busted down the door to the closet. Inside they found SuperSpy X tied to a chair with a gag in his mouth so he couldn't call for help!

"X, what happened?" asked Q after they untied the prisoner.

"It's Doc Rotten! He snuck into our secret headquarters and knocked me out."

"He's pretending to be SuperSpy D!" cried T.

"And he's got my sister!" yelled Q.

The SuperSpies had to act fast. They jumped into their SpyShuttles and used their tracking rays to find SuperSpies M and K9.

But when they found the SuperSpies, the action was over. M and K9 had Doc Rotten wrapped in SpyNets, and they were waiting for the police.

"K9 knew D was a fake as soon as she saw him," said M, patting K9 on the head.

"How did she know?" asked Q.

"She could tell by the smell!" said M. "Superdogs make SuperSpies!"

Now, NUMBER the events to show the order in which they happened.

HINT: The events are listed the way they were told to you, not necessarily in the order they happened.

_____ SuperSpy D took M and K9 away.

_____ Q found X locked in a closet.

_____ Doc Rotten snuck into the SpyStation and knocked out X.

_____ The SuperSpies found M and K9.

_____ M and K9 overpowered Doc Rotten

and tied him up.

_____ K9 knew right away that D

was really Doc Rotten.

Story Plan

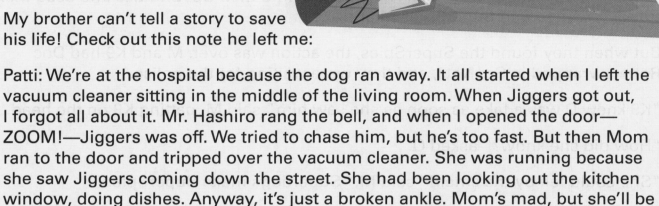

READ the story.

A Mixed Up Story

My brother can't tell a story to save his life! Check out this note he left me:

Patti: We're at the hospital because the dog ran away. It all started when I left the vacuum cleaner sitting in the middle of the living room. When Jiggers got out, I forgot all about it. Mr. Hashiro rang the bell, and when I opened the door—ZOOM!—Jiggers was off. We tried to chase him, but he's too fast. But then Mom ran to the door and tripped over the vacuum cleaner. She was running because she saw Jiggers coming down the street. She had been looking out the kitchen window, doing dishes. Anyway, it's just a broken ankle. Mom's mad, but she'll be fine. And Jiggers is locked in the basement. I found him sitting on the front steps.

—Kyle

Kyle messed up the order of his story. Can you put it back together? NUMBER the events to show the order in which they happened.

_____ Kyle and Mr. Hashiro chased after him.

_____ Kyle was vacuuming when the doorbell rang.

_____ Meanwhile, Mom was in the kitchen doing dishes when she saw Jiggers coming down the street.

_____ Kyle found Jiggers sitting on the front steps and locked him in the basement before going with his mom to the hospital.

_____ She ran through the living room, tripped over the vacuum and broke her ankle.

_____ Kyle opened the door and Jiggers the dog ran away.

Some articles have a lot of information. They may have more than one main idea. But every article should have one BIG IDEA. So to keep track of your facts in longer articles, look for the big idea, then the main ideas, then all the details. Don't worry—everything will fall into place! In this mind map, FIND the big idea at the top and the main ideas in the circles. FILL IN the details (in the boxes).

World Cup	Olympic Finals	goalie
Real Madrid	LA Galaxy	Manchester United
midfielder	center	African Cup

Soccer

Positions
1. _____
2. _____
3. _____

Big Games
1. _____
2. _____
3. _____

Teams
1. _____
2. _____
3. _____

FIND the big idea at the top. FILL IN the circles with the main ideas. Then FILL IN the details under each main idea with the details in the box.

palomino   oats   pony   hay
jumping   bridle   carrots   riding
saddle   mustang   racing   reins

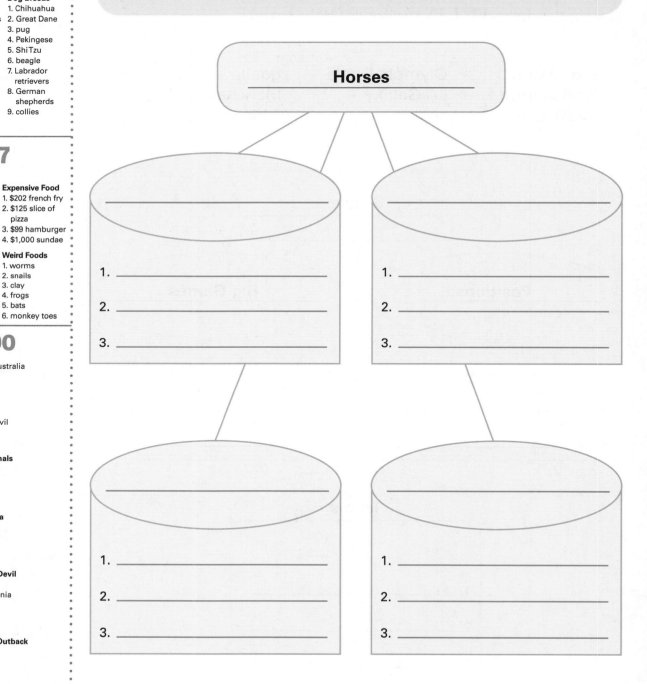

What's the BIG IDEA? Figure it out! FILL IN all the blanks in this mind map!

HINT: Sort the details, and count how many are in each set.

cruise ship   SUV   truck   sailboat   jeep   ferry   train
space shuttle   subway   helicopter   airplane   canoe   bus   car

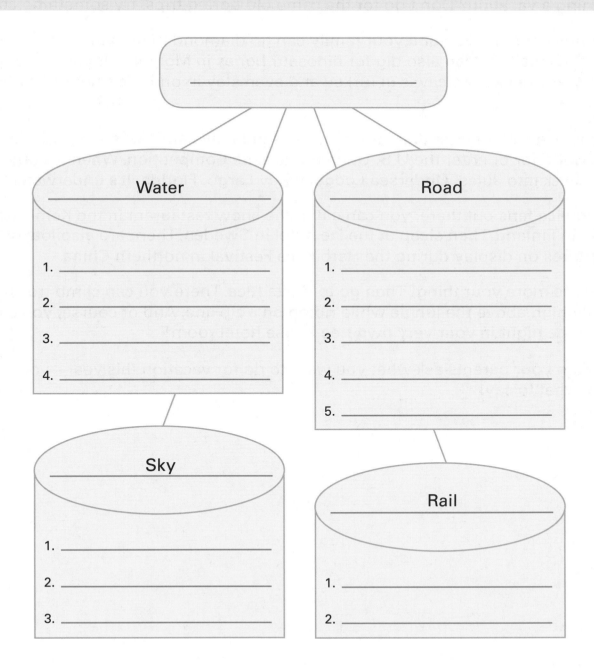

Water
1. _____
2. _____
3. _____
4. _____

Road
1. _____
2. _____
3. _____
4. _____
5. _____

Sky
1. _____
2. _____
3. _____

Rail
1. _____
2. _____

READ this article, and then MAP it!

Gotta Go!

Planning a vacation? Don't go for the same old boring trips. Try something cool!

Did you know that you and your family can go diamond mining in Pennsylvania? You can also dig for dinosaur bones in Montana. If you like to get dirty, you can explore caves in Turkey and even stay in one. It's true! Turkey has *two* cave hotels!

Do you like water better than dirt? You can scuba dive and see shipwrecks in Lake Superior or enter the U.S. Open Sandcastle Competition. When it's time for bed, check into Jules' Undersea Lodge in Key Largo, Florida. It's underwater!

For you ice fans out there, you can eat at the snow restaurant in the Kemi snow castle in Finland. Then sleep at the ice hotel in Sweden. There are also lots of ice sculptures on display during the Harbin Ice Festival in northern China.

Are trees more your thing? Then go to Costa Rica. There you can climb trees and fly high above the jungle while riding on a zip line. And of course, you can spend the night in your very own tree house hotel room!

So when your parents ask what you want to do for vacation this year—you know what to say!

Now, FILL IN the mind map for the article you just read.

Cool Vacations
_____

Funky Hotels
_____

1. _____

2. _____

3. _____

4. _____

Countries to Visit
_____

1. _____

2. _____

3. _____

4. _____

5. _____

6. _____

Things to Do
_____

1. _____

2. _____

3. _____

4. _____

5. _____

6. _____

7. _____

8. _____

9. _____

READ this article, and then MAP it!

The Wolf in Your House

Believe it or not, every dog is part wolf. That's right! There are more than 400 breeds of dog, from the tiny Chihuahua to the giant Great Dane. But each one evolved from the wild wolf.

Dogs and wolves are different in lots of ways. Dogs have smaller brains than wolves, because they don't need to hunt. But that doesn't mean they're stupid! In fact, dogs are better at figuring out human behavior. Dogs also have shorter snouts and smaller teeth than wolves. (It's easier to eat out of a bowl if you have a short snout!) But the main difference between a wild wolf and a tame dog is that a wolf isn't comfortable around humans, while most dogs love living with us!

People breed different kinds of dogs to do different jobs. Small dogs like pugs, Pekingese, and Shih Tzus were made to be the perfect lap dogs. Dogs like beagles and Labrador retrievers are great at hunting. And German shepherds and collies are experts at herding sheep!

The bad part about breeding is that over time some breeds have developed major health problems. Dogs with lots of wrinkles get skin infections, really small dogs have heart problems, and really large dogs have hip problems. Dogs with smooshed noses may have trouble breathing. Plus, dogs who were born to do outdoor jobs (like catching rats or herding animals) may go a little crazy just hanging around the house.

If you're looking for a pet, try your local animal shelter. They might not have any fancy breeds, but they'll have some smart, healthy mutts!

Now, FILL IN the mind map.

```
        ┌─────────────────────────┐
        │   _____  │
        └─────────────────────────┘
```

Dogs vs. Wolves _____

1. _____

2. _____

3. _____

4. _____

5. _____

Breed Illnesses _____

1. _____

2. _____

3. _____

4. _____

5. _____

Dog Breeds _____

1. _____

2. _____

3. _____

4. _____

5. _____

6. _____

7. _____

8. _____

9. _____

READ this article, and then MAP it!

Food Play

Everybody's got to eat, right? But some people eat the craziest things!

When it comes to food, we like it *big*. Sometimes, it grows that way. One farm in Oregon grows giant pumpkins, weighing more than half a ton. What do you do with a pumpkin that big? Drop it on a car of course! They do it every year.

When you're making things big, it's good to stick to yummy foods—like a chocolate chip cookie that's 100 feet in diameter. That's the size of a basketball court! It took six hours to bake in a special oven. Would you like a Hershey Kiss that is 6,340 pounds of dark chocolate? And get this: The world's longest french fry (over six feet long!) was sold online for $202!

Speaking of prices, would you pay $125 for a slice of pizza (topped with caviar and lobster)? Or $99 for a hamburger (with fancy truffles and foie gras)? Hold on to your hats—at Serendipity in New York City, the Grand Opulence Sundae costs $1,000! It's covered in edible gold.

Some people think food can be an edible masterpiece. The Godiva company has an entire room made out of chocolate. Jim Victor is a food sculptor who carved a farm out of cheese (including a cow). And in London, some movie fans made a statue of King Kong that stood 13 feet tall—entirely out of popcorn!

Food is one of those things people can never agree about. In some parts of the world it's cool to eat worms, snails, clay, frogs, bats, and monkey toes! You think that's weird, huh? Well, have you ever read the ingredients of your favorite foods?

Now, FILL IN the mind map.

Big Food _____

1. _____
2. _____
3. _____
4. _____

Expensive Food _____

1. _____
2. _____
3. _____
4. _____

Food Art _____

1. _____
2. _____
3. _____

Weird Foods _____

1. _____
2. _____
3. _____
4. _____
5. _____
6. _____

READ this article, and then MAP it!

Awesome Australia

The country of Australia is a land like no other. It's filled with unusual, dangerous, and amazing animals!

Australia is most famous for its *marsupials*. Marsupials are mammals, and the females have a pouch where they carry their babies. You can probably name at least one marsupial: the kangaroo! There's also the koala bear, the bandicoot, the Tasmanian devil, the wallaby, and the Quokka!

Let's take a closer look at the Tasmanian devil. It's nothing like the cartoon! The devil is a little black-furred animal that lives on the island of Tasmania, which is a state of Australia. It's famous for its bad smell, strong bite, and eerie scream when it feels cornered.

But in a country with so many dangerous animals, the devil isn't scary at all! Australia has more poisonous snakes than any other country. It's also home to many great white sharks. And don't forget the world's largest reptile: the saltwater crocodile. But even deadlier than snakes, sharks, or crocodiles is the box jellyfish. That's right! The box jellyfish has a poison on its tentacles that can stop a human heart in about three minutes. Eek!

In Australia's desert, the *outback*, you'll find wild dogs called *dingoes*, which were introduced to Australia about 3,500 years ago. They're like wolves. And guess what? Camels were brought to Australia around 1840. They were perfect for carrying stuff across the outback for settlers. Camels that escaped from captivity started breeding, and now almost a million of them live in the wild!

But if you want to see something really amazing, look up! Australia's skies are filled with beautiful parrots: lorikeets, cockatoos, and Budgerigars. These birds aren't living in cages; this is their home turf! But the largest bird in Australia doesn't fly. The Emu is like an ostrich. It lays dark green eggs that are bigger than hockey pucks.

If you like animals, Australia's the place to visit!

TURN the page to MAP the article.

Mind Maps

FILL IN the mind map for the article you just read.

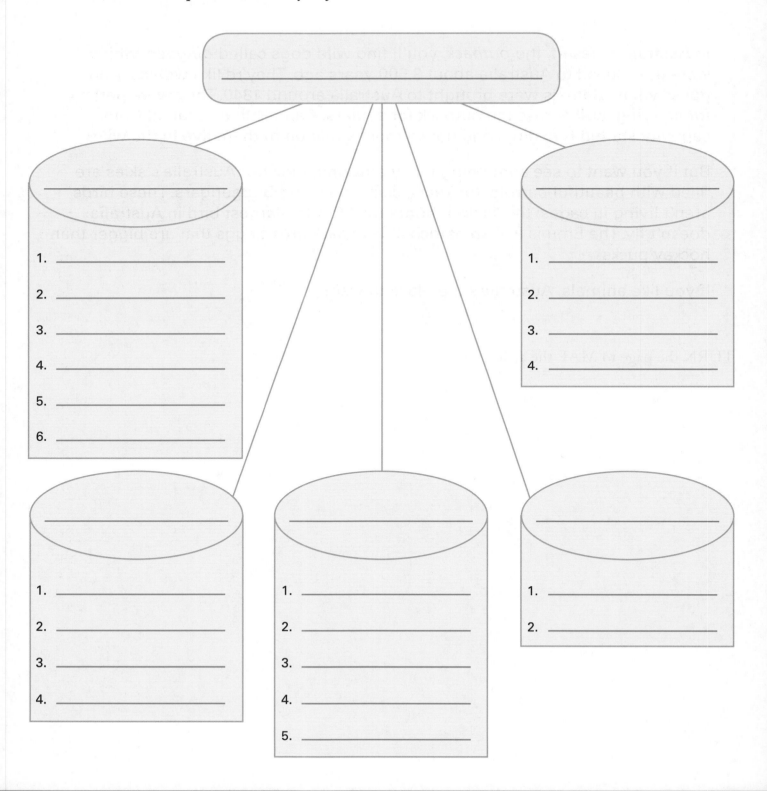

Story Plan

PICK a story you've finished reading. Then FILL OUT this worksheet.

Name of story _____

Main character _____

Character details _____

The setting _____

The problem _____
_____

Event _____
_____

Event _____
_____

Event _____
_____

The solution _____
_____

Story Plan

PICK a story you've finished reading. Then FILL OUT this worksheet.

Name of story

Main character _____

Character details _____

The setting _____

The problem _____

_____

Event _____

_____

Event _____

_____

Event _____

_____

The solution _____

_____

Mind Maps

PICK a nonfiction book or article you've finished reading. Then MAP IT here.

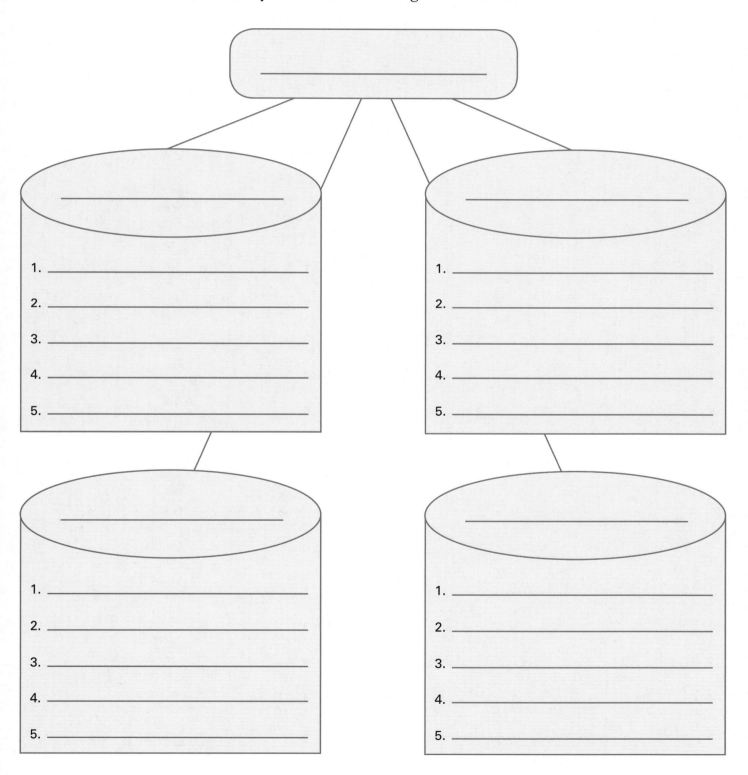

Mind Maps

PICK a nonfiction book or article you've finished reading. Then MAP IT here.

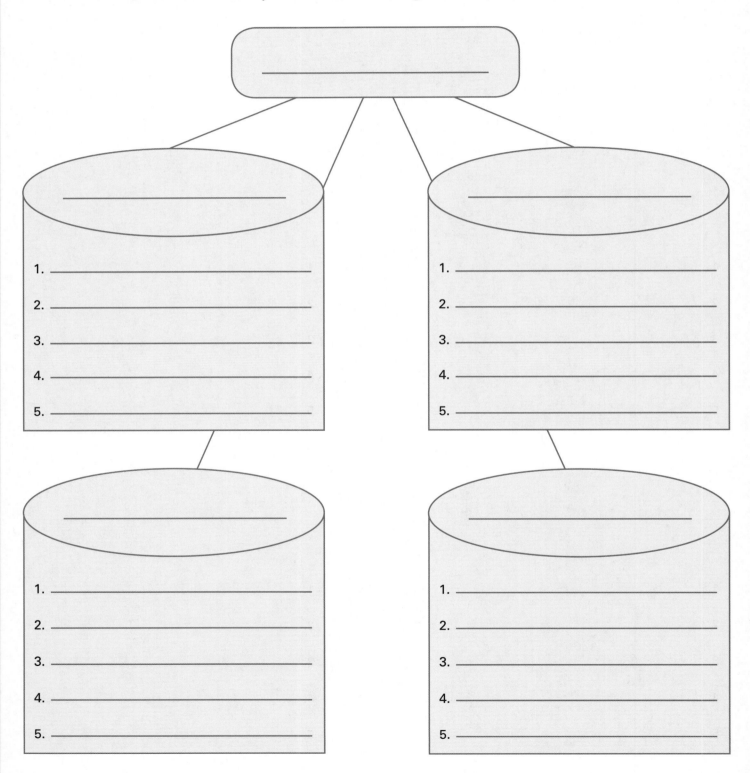

Stop & Go Story

Are you ready to practice all your new skills? READ the story and FILL IN the blanks along the way.

 GO

Alberto and the Magic Teapot

 STOP 1. What do you think this story is about?

_____

2. **What kind of story is it?**
(Circle one)

romance   mystery

fantasy   comedy

 GO

Alberto loved trash! He could dig in a dumpster all day long. And anyway, it got him out of the house. Alberto's house was really sad right now. His mom was sick and his dad was worried. So Alberto hit the streets of his little town and hunted for treasures in the trash.

 STOP

3. What is Alberto's problem? _____

_____

 GO

One day, Alberto was digging around in a dumpster behind Old Man Garcia's junk shop. Hey! Alberto found a teapot. It was dirty, but it looked like gold underneath the grime. His mother loved tea. So Alberto decided to clean it up and bring it to her.

4. **What do you think will happen next?**

_____

_____

Check It!

GO

Alberto found a rag and rubbed the teapot really hard. The teapot began to shine. Then it began to buzz! Then it started to spin! As it spun on the floor, a puff of green smoke came out of its spout. The smoke got bigger and greener and turned into a genie!

STOP

5. Now what do you think will happen next?

_____

_____

"I am the genie of the teapot," said the genie, who was fat and had green skin. He sat cross-legged, floating above the floor.

"What does genie mean?" asked Alberto.

"It means I grant wishes to whoever rubs the teapot," said the genie, "but only when I'm in a good mood."

"Are you in a good mood now?" asked Alberto.

"Not really."

6. Now what do you think will happen next?

_____

_____

GO

"What can I do to make you happy?" asked Alberto.

The genie thought for a minute. "You can wish for me to have a party with all my genie friends."

So Alberto made the wish. Suddenly his bedroom was filled with genies. There was a girl genie with blue skin and long black hair and another fat man genie with red skin. An old lady genie started playing a guitar. Soon all the genies were singing and eating cake. None of them touched the ground—they just floated around!

Now DRAW the genie party in the box below.

STOP

Review

 STOP Before you keep reading, answer this question: What do you think *cantankerous* means?

_____

 GO The genie party lasted most of the night. Alberto slept downstairs on the couch. The next morning, the genie was feeling cantankerous. No matter what Alberto did, the genie got mad. He threw breakfast across the room. He broke Alberto's video game console. And he wouldn't grant any wishes.

"No way," said the genie, shaking his head. "I'm in a bad mood."

STOP READ the context questions, and CIRCLE the correct answers.

7. How is *cantankerous* being used here?
   a. It's a noun.
   b. It's a verb.
   c. It's an adjective.

8. How does a cantankerous genie act?
   a. Silly and sweet
   b. Angry and mean
   c. Sad and sleepy

9. When will the genie grant a wish?
   a. When he's in a good mood
   b. When his stomach is full of good food
   c. When Alberto plays him music

10. Will the genie grant a wish while he's feeling cantankerous?
    a. Yes
    b. No

11. What's another word for *cantankerous*?
    a. Happy
    b. Depressed
    c. Grouchy

GO

Now Alberto was getting tired of this useless genie.

"All right!" he said to the genie. "It's time for you to grant my wish."

"I don't know," said the genie, eating some potato chips out of the bag. "I'm feeling a little tired. You better wish for me to have a two-week vacation in Hawaii. I'll help you out when I get back."

STOP

12. What's Alberto's new problem? _____

_____

GO

"Okay," said Alberto. "I'm going to make the wish. Are you ready?"

The genie sucked in his big belly and nodded. "Ready!"

"Okay. I wish . . . I wish for a different genie!"

The genie had to grant Alberto's wish. That's the rule.

So POOF! The big, green, grumpy genie was replaced by a new, blue, frumpy genie.

"Your wish is my command," said the new genie.

Alberto smiled. Finally he could make his wish! "I wish that—"

Suddenly Alberto's dad called to him. "Alberto, come quick! Mami is feeling well again, and she wants to play dominos with you."

"Gotta go," Alberto told the genie. Then he raced out of the room.

13. How did Alberto solve his new problem? _____

_____

14. How was Alberto's old problem solved? _____

_____

15. What is the title of the story you just read? _____

16. Who is the main character of the story? _____

Now, WRITE a summary of the story by telling what happened, in order.

17. What happened first? _____

_____

18. Then what happened? _____

_____

19. Then what happened? _____

_____

20. What happened at the end? _____

_____

What did you think about the story? What did you think about the characters, the

problem, and the solution? _____

_____

_____

Would you tell your friends to read this story? Circle one: YES   NO

Why or why not? _____

_____

_____

_____

Stop & Go Story

Now it's time to practice your skills reading nonfiction!

READ the article that starts on the next page. But first, PREPARE to read, and FILL IN the blanks along the way.

GO

The Future––Today!

Table of Contents

STOP

From the table of contents, what do you think the article will be about?

1. _____

2. _____

3. _____

4. _____

What do you already know about these topics?

5. _____

_____

_____

✓ Check It!

Page 111

Stop & Go Story

1. robots
2. cars
3. space tourists
4. flying
5. **Suggestions:** Robots are made of metal. Cars can run on electricity.

Page 112

Stop & Go Story

Suggestions:
6. Robots will someday work in the home as lawn mowers, security guards, or window-washers. Humanoid robots look like humans and aren't practical.

Page 113

Stop & Go Story

Suggestions:
7. Humanoid robots can be dancing partners, soccer players, or companions to the elderly.
8. There are self-driving cars and automated highway systems in the works.
9. There are three companies working on flying cars.

Page 114

Stop & Go Story

1. a
2. a
3. c
4. b
5. b

Check It!

Page 115

Stop & Go Story

Main Idea 1: The Future of Air Travel

Subtopic 1: Problems
1. high fuel costs
2. pollution
3. too many passengers

Subtopic 2: Solutions
1. change airplane shape
2. fly slower and lower
3. bigger planes
4. microjets

Page 116

Big Idea: The Future

Main Idea 1: Robot Jobs

Subtopic 1: Nonhumanoid
1. vacuum
2. lawn mower
3. security guard
4. window washer
5. disaster rescue

Subtopic 2: Humanoid
1. dance partner
2. soccer player
3. companion

Main Idea 2: Cars

Subtopic 1: The Future of Driving
1. self-driving cars
2. automated highway systems

Subtopic 2: Flying Car Makers
1. Moller International
2. LaBiche Aerospace
3. Boeing

Main idea 3: Space Tourism

Subtopic 1: Reasons to Go to Space
1. break through atmosphere
2. see Earth from space
3. zero gravity

Subtopic 2: Who Will Take You
1. Russian Space Agency
2. Virgin Galactic

GO

The future is now! We've got robots, cars that can drive themselves, and a growing space travel industry. Almost everything you could imagine already exists or is right around the corner.

Today robots have jobs on the battlefield, in the factory, and in outer space. At home you'll mostly find robots as vacuum cleaners. But that will change. Lawn mowers might be next, as well as robot security guards or window-washers. But you won't see too many robots assuming human form. A *humanoid* robot isn't practical. It's easier to engineer a boxy robot that runs on wheels.

STOP

6. What did you just learn about robots?

_____

_____

GO

But why be practical? In Japan, they've developed a robot that looks like a bright pink girl in a ball gown. What's her job? Ballroom dance partner, of course! Humanoid robots play soccer in the RoboCup Soccer tournament every year. The goal of the RoboCup team is to create an all-robot soccer team that could beat a human one. They also develop nonhumanoid robots to work in disaster rescues. The Mitsubishi company sells a "companion" robot called Wakamaru that's designed to hang out with people who are elderly or sick.

STOP

7. What did you just learn about robots?

_____

_____

GO

Word on the street is that major car companies are working on cars that can drive themselves! It's not as new as you think. In 2005, four self-driving cars finished a 132-mile race in the desert in less than 10 hours. Engineers are also creating _automated highway systems_—special lanes on the highway that use laser beams, magnets, and computers to manage traffic while the passengers sit back and relax!

STOP

8. What did you just learn about cars? _____

_____

Even cooler than a car that drives itself is a car that can fly, right? When it's finished, the SkyCar from Moller International will have a cool cockpit and four jet propellers like an airplane. The FSC-1 from LaBiche Aerospace looks more like a car with wings. The wings fold up and tuck away so you can drive it like usual. Even famous airplane builder Boeing is in the mix. They have a team looking into a combination helicopter and car (a "helicar"?). Keep your eyes on the skies!

9. What did you just learn about cars? _____

_____

Stop & Go Story

READ the story and FILL IN the blanks along the way.

 Before you read the story, answer this question: What do you think the

word *exhilaration* means?

_____

 Believe it or not, there are people who will spend millions of dollars just for the exhilaration of a trip to space. Why should astronauts have all the fun? Space tourists want to break through the atmosphere, see the Earth from space, and float in zero gravity. The Russian Space Agency has been taking up tourists in their Soyuz rockets since 2001. Now Virgin Galactic is booking trips on their own privately built SpaceShipTwo. Want a ticket?

 READ the context questions, and CIRCLE the correct answers.

1. How is *exhilaration* being used here?
   a. It's a noun.
   b. It's a verb.
   c. It's an adjective.

2. How are space tourists getting exhilaration?
   a. Taking a spaceship ride
   b. Watching TV
   c. Paying a lot of money

3. What does the exhilaration of a space trip include?
   a. Comfy seats and quiet music
   b. Jokes and laughter
   c. Breaking the atmosphere and floating in zero gravity

4. Would exhilaration make you sleepy?
   a. Yes
   b. No

5. What's another word for *exhilaration*?
   a. Joy
   b. Thrill
   c. Inconvenience

Space tourism aside, the future of air travel centers on solving three big problems: high fuel costs, pollution, and too many passengers. Changing the shape of airplanes may help in one area. The traditional "tube and wing" shape has been used forever. But engineers are starting to look at a shape that blends body and wing like a manta-ray, or the Bat Plane. This new shape will enable planes to use less fuel and be quieter at the same time. Planes may also fly slower and lower in the future. Crazy, huh? But it might help use less fuel and reduce pollution.

What about the passenger problem? One idea is to make planes bigger. The new Airbus A-380 will hold 555 passengers (today's airplanes hold about 400). But that means *lots* more people will jam the major airports. So other companies are building microjets, smaller, lighter airplanes that will take people from one community airport to another. It's like taking an air taxi!

STOP Fill in the details under the main idea.

Main Idea 1: The Future of Air Travel

Subtopic 1: Problems

Details:

1. _____

2. _____

3. _____

Subtopic 2: Solutions

Details:

1. _____

2. _____

3. _____

4. _____

Now, FILL IN the mind map for the article you just read.

HINT: Go back and look at each paragraph to find the main ideas and subtopics.

_____

Subtopic 1

_____

1. _____

2. _____

3. _____

4. _____

5. _____

Subtopic 2

_____

1. _____

2. _____

3. _____

_____

Subtopic 1

_____

1. _____

2. _____

Subtopic 2

_____

1. _____

2. _____

3. _____

_____

Subtopic 1

_____

1. _____

2. _____

3. _____

Subtopic 2

_____

1. _____

2. _____

Fiction Book Notes

PICK a story you've finished reading. Then FILL OUT this worksheet.

The setting of the story is _____

_____

_____ is a character who

_____ .

Another character in the story is _____

who _____

_____ .

The problem happens when _____

_____

_____ .

Then, _____

_____ .

and then,_____

_____ .

The solution _____

_____

_____ .

Finally, _____

_____

_____ .

Fiction Book Notes

PICK a story you've finished reading. Then FILL OUT this worksheet.

The setting of the story is _____

_____

_____ is a character who

_____.

Another character in the story is _____

who _____

_____.

The problem happens when _____

_____

_____.

Then, _____

_____

and then, _____

_____.

The solution _____

_____

_____.

Finally, _____

_____

_____.

Nonfiction Book Notes

PICK a nonfiction article you've finished reading. Then FILL OUT this worksheet.

What is this article about? _____

_____

_____

What did you learn from this article? _____

_____

Fill in the main ideas and details of this article:

_____   _____

_____   _____

_____   _____

What did you think about this article? _____

_____

_____

Was this article easy or hard to understand? Why? _____

_____

Would you recommend this article to a friend? Circle one: YES   NO

Why? Why not? _____

_____

_____

Nonfiction Book Notes

PICK a nonfiction article you've finished reading. Then FILL OUT this worksheet.

What is this article about? _____

_____

_____

What did you learn from this article? _____

_____

Fill in the main ideas and details of this article:

_____   _____

_____   _____

_____   _____

What did you think about this article? _____

_____

_____

Was this article easy or hard to understand? Why? _____

_____

Would you recommend this article to a friend? Circle one: YES   NO

Why? Why not?_____

_____

_____

3rd Grade
Basic Math Success

Contents

Contents

Find Your Place

IDENTIFY the place of each digit. Then WRITE the digit.

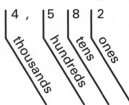

Example:

9,214

Commas make numbers easier to read. A comma belongs after the thousands place.

ones	4
tens	1
hundreds	2
thousands	9

1. **1,805**

ones _____

tens _____

hundreds _____

thousands _____

2. **7,336**

ones _____

tens _____

hundreds _____

thousands _____

3. **8,240**

ones _____

tens _____

hundreds _____

thousands _____

4. **3,699**

ones _____

tens _____

hundreds _____

thousands _____

5. **6,002**

ones _____

tens _____

hundreds _____

thousands _____

6. **2,173**

ones _____

tens _____

hundreds _____

thousands _____

Place Value

Number Words

WRITE the number words.

HINT: A comma goes after the thousands in the written form of the number, just like in the number itself.

Example: 8,172   8,172 in written form is
              eight thousand, one hundred seventy-two.

1. 6,405   six thousand, four hundred five

2. 1,538

3. 2,780

4. 4,999

5. 7,263

6. 9,314

WRITE the number.

7. three thousand, five hundred seventy-six   3,576

8. eight thousand, six hundred thirty-three

9. five thousand, two hundred ten

10. nine thousand, eight hundred ninety-one

11. seven thousand, three hundred forty-five

12. one thousand, four hundred fifty-two

Get in Place

WRITE how many thousands, hundreds, tens, and ones you see. Then WRITE the number.

1.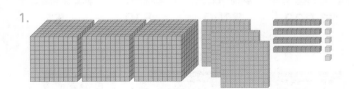

Thousands	Hundreds	Tens	Ones

= _____

2.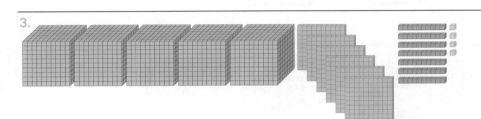

Thousands	Hundreds	Tens	Ones

= _____

3.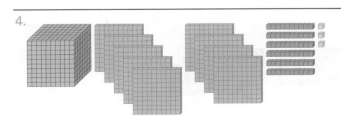

Thousands	Hundreds	Tens	Ones

= _____

4.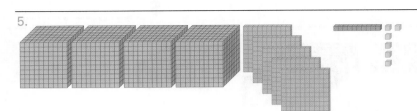

Thousands	Hundreds	Tens	Ones

= _____

5.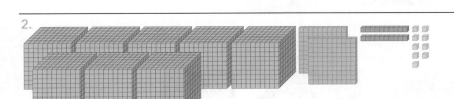

Thousands	Hundreds	Tens	Ones

= _____

6.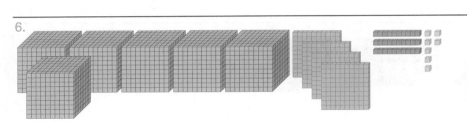

Thousands	Hundreds	Tens	Ones

= _____

Place Value

Money's Worth

WRITE how much money you see in each picture.

$1,000 $100 $10 $1

1.

$ _____ , _____

2.

$ _____ , _____

3.

$ _____ , _____

4.

$ _____ , _____

5.

$ _____ , _____

6.

$ _____ , _____

Mismatched

WRITE > or < in each box.

650 **<** 825
1

503 ☐ 490
2

239 ☐ 223
3

2,879 ☐ 4,923
4

6,067 ☐ 8,489
5

7,445 ☐ 6,301
6

5,636 ☐ 5,207
7

2,389 ☐ 3,289
8

9,591 ☐ 9,958
9

6,892 ☐ 6,799
10

3,140 ☐ 3,410
11

1,655 ☐ 1,556
12

9,008 ☐ 9,001
13

4,128 ☐ 4,182
14

3,372 ☐ 3,374
15

Matched or Mismatched?

WRITE >, <, or = in each box.

1. $3,822

2. $2,569

3. $5,282

4. $9,177

5. $6,408

6. $7,325

Which One?

CIRCLE the largest number in each row.

1. 4,285   1,290   3,534   6,672

2. 9,158   6,923   7,227   8,831

3. 5,746   4,955   5,803   5,069

4. 4,890   4,385   4,761   4,910

5. 7,398   7,374   7,212   7,356

6. 3,841   3,848   3,840   3,835

Which One?

CIRCLE the smallest number in each row.

1.	5,208	4,763	8,459	5,530
2.	7,848	8,125	7,957	8,002
3.	3,491	4,862	3,399	4,153
4.	6,589	6,332	6,912	6,474
5.	2,174	2,238	2,634	2,165
6.	9,530	9,602	9,592	9,528

Round About

Rounding makes numbers easier to work with.

Numbers that end in 1 through 4 get rounded **down** to the nearest ten.

Numbers that end in 5 through 9 get rounded **up** to the nearest ten.

Numbers that end in 1 through 49 get rounded **down** to the nearest hundred.

Numbers that end in 50 through 99 get rounded **up** to the nearest hundred.

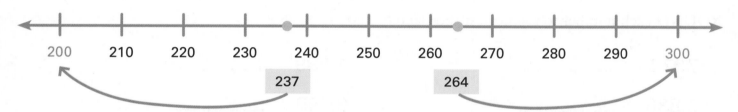

ROUND each number to the nearest ten.

1. 22 _____
2. 87 _____
3. 41 _____
4. 94 _____

5. 53 _____
6. 78 _____
7. 16 _____
8. 35 _____

ROUND each number to the nearest hundred.

9. 504 _____
10. 367 _____
11. 129 _____
12. 781 _____

13. 472 _____
14. 831 _____
15. 644 _____
16. 256 _____

Round About

Rounding large numbers works the same way.

Numbers that end in 1 through 499 get rounded **down** to the nearest thousand.

Numbers that end in 500 through 999 get rounded **up** to the nearest thousand.

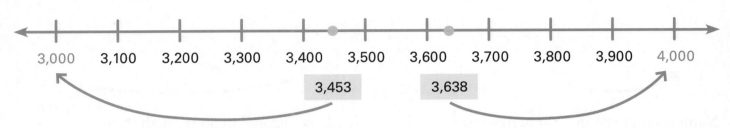

3,453

3,638

ROUND each number to the nearest thousand.

1. 7,372 _____

2. 1,239 _____

3. 5,836 _____

4. 8,199 _____

5. 2,964 _____

6. 6,078 _____

7. 8,735 _____

8. 3,484 _____

9. 1,577 _____

10. 4,179 _____

11. 7,991 _____

12. 5,639 _____

13. 3,743 _____

14. 2,804 _____

15. 6,529 _____

16. 4,495 _____

Guess and Check

Estimating is making a reasonable guess about something. ESTIMATE the amount of money in each set. Then CHECK your guess by counting the money.

1. Estimate: _____

   Check: _____

2. Estimate: _____

   Check: _____

3. Estimate: _____

   Check: _____

Loop It

ESTIMATE the number of bees. Then CIRCLE groups of 10 to count the bees and check your estimate.

Estimate: _____   Check: _____

Write the Number

WRITE the number or number words.

1. eight thousand, four hundred twenty-one   _____

2. three thousand, nine hundred fifty-four   _____

3. five thousand, seven hundred thirty-six   _____

4. seven thousand, six hundred seventy-seven   _____

5. 4,385   _____

6. 6,509   _____

7. 7,138   _____

8. 9,870   _____

Use all of the numbers above to answer each question. WRITE the number.

9. Which number has a 1 in the ones place?   _____

10. Which number has an 8 in the tens place?   _____

11. Which number has a 5 in the tens place?   _____

12. Which number has a 5 in the thousands place?   _____

13. Which number has a 3 in the hundreds place?   _____

14. Which number has a 9 in the thousands place?   _____

Unit Rewind

1. CIRCLE the largest number.

   8,730   8,802   8,810   8,797

2. CIRCLE the smallest number.

   5,187   5,214   5,199   5,239

   ROUND each number to the nearest hundred.

   672 _____   904 _____   853 _____   248 _____
   ₃   ₄   ₅   ₆

   ROUND each number to the nearest thousand.

   5,927 _____   1,256 _____   6,510 _____   3,445 _____
   ₇   ₈   ₉   ₁₀

11. ESTIMATE the number of stars. Then COUNT to check your estimate.

   Estimate: _____   Check: _____

It All Adds Up

WRITE each sum.

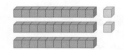 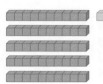

1. **32** + **51** = _____

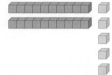 

2. **25** + **33** = _____

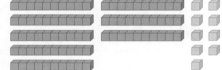

3. **89** + **10** = _____

 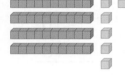

4. **46** + **21** = _____

5. 74
   + 13

6. 27
   + 22

7. 61
   + 32

8. 23
   + 43

9. 38
   + 21

10. 16
    + 32

11. 26
    + 50

12. 71
    + 26

Adding & Subtracting 2-Digit Numbers

What's the Difference?

WRITE each difference.

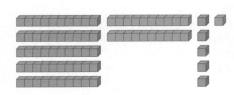

1. 76 – 21 = _____

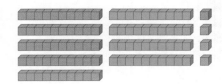

2. 94 – 53 = _____

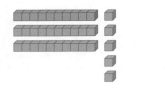

3. 35 – 25 = _____

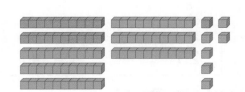

4. 87 – 66 = _____

5. 88
  – 41

6. 28
  – 13

7. 84
  – 52

8. 96
  – 43

9. 79
  – 48

10. 48
  – 22

11. 98
  – 30

12. 65
  – 53

It All Adds Up

WRITE each sum.

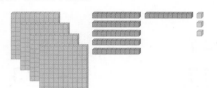

1. 463 + 126 = _____

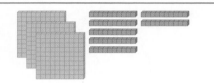 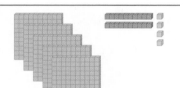

2. 370 + 524 = _____

 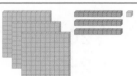

3. 314 + 244 = _____

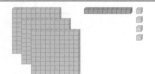 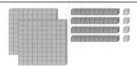

4. 136 + 331 = _____

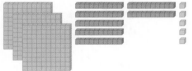 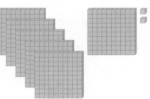

5. 375 + 602 = _____

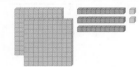 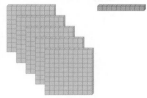

6. 232 + 510 = _____

It All Adds Up

WRITE each sum.

1.
```
  415
+  32
```

2.
```
  128
+  51
```

3.
```
  341
+  15
```

4.
```
  822
+  73
```

5.
```
  656
+  43
```

6.
```
  532
+  20
```

7.
```
  732
+  16
```

8.
```
  904
+  65
```

9.
```
  231
+ 542
```

10.
```
  204
+ 292
```

11.
```
  824
+ 125
```

12.
```
  160
+ 137
```

13.
```
  451
+ 213
```

14.
```
  364
+ 221
```

15.
```
  191
+ 603
```

16.
```
  342
+ 134
```

Pick Apart

Partial sums is a method of addition, adding each place one at a time.

		6 6 4
		+ 2 5 8
Add the numbers in the hundreds place.	600 + 200 =	8 0 0
Add the numbers in the tens place.	60 + 50 =	1 1 0
Add the numbers in the ones place.	4 + 8 =	+ 1 2
Then add the numbers together.		9 2 2

WRITE each sum using partial sums.

1.
```
   516
 + 349
```

2.
```
   399
 + 174
```

3.
```
   472
 + 225
```

4.
```
   534
 + 177
```

5.
```
   290
 + 636
```

6.
```
   198
 + 184
```

7.
```
   427
 + 296
```

8.
```
   688
 + 263
```

It All Adds Up

WRITE each sum.

564 + 278	First, add the ones. 4 + 8 = 12	¹ 564 + 278 ——— 2	Write a 2 in the ones place, and a 1 in the tens place. Add the tens. 1 + 6 + 7 = 14.	¹ ¹ 564 + 278 ——— 42	Write a 4 in the tens place, and a 1 in the hundreds place. Add the hundreds. 1 + 5 + 2 = 8	¹ ¹ 564 + 278 ——— 842	Write an 8 in the hundreds place.

1.
$$726$$
$$+\ 185$$

2.
$$348$$
$$+\ 297$$

3.
$$198$$
$$+\ 593$$

4.
$$460$$
$$+\ 323$$

5.
$$173$$
$$+\ 248$$

6.
$$176$$
$$+\ 329$$

7.
$$655$$
$$+\ 177$$

8.
$$256$$
$$+\ 256$$

9.
$$803$$
$$+\ 129$$

10.
$$452$$
$$+\ 368$$

11.
$$457$$
$$+\ 243$$

12.
$$369$$
$$+\ 288$$

What's the Difference?

WRITE each difference.

1. **473** — **321** = _____

2. **549** — **126** = _____

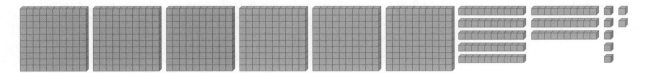

3. **687** — **382** = _____

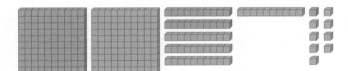

4. **269** — **148** = _____

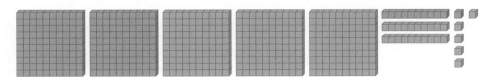

5. **536** — **325** = _____

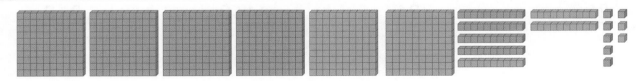

6. **678** — **232** = _____

Subtracting 3-Digit Numbers

What's the Difference?

WRITE each difference.

1.
$$738$$
$$-\ 24$$

2.
$$393$$
$$-\ 41$$

3.
$$896$$
$$-\ 72$$

4.
$$545$$
$$-\ 32$$

5.
$$983$$
$$-722$$

6.
$$878$$
$$-316$$

7.
$$569$$
$$-127$$

8.
$$466$$
$$-362$$

9.
$$348$$
$$-211$$

10.
$$419$$
$$-101$$

11.
$$784$$
$$-453$$

12.
$$878$$
$$-357$$

13.
$$928$$
$$-223$$

14.
$$695$$
$$-321$$

15.
$$869$$
$$-440$$

16.
$$893$$
$$-213$$

What's the Difference?

WRITE each difference.

1.   342   –   158   = _____

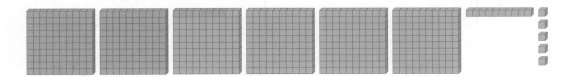

2.   615   –   407   = _____

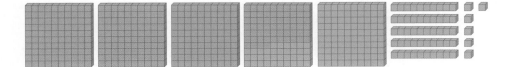

3.   556   –   192   = _____

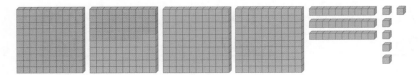

4.   436   –   288   = _____

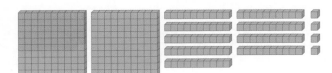

5.   294   –   235   = _____

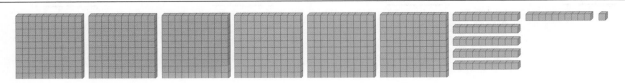

6.   661   –   372   = _____

Subtracting 3-Digit Numbers

What's the Difference?

WRITE each difference.

| $\overset{5\ 14}{8\cancel{6}\cancel{4}}$ $-\ 577$ | First, regroup ten from the tens place. Cross out 6 and write 5, and cross out 4 and write 14. | $\overset{5\ 14}{8\cancel{6}\cancel{4}}$ $-\ 577$ $\overline{\quad\ 7}$ | Subtract in the ones place: $14 - 7 = 7$. Write 7 in the ones place. | $\overset{7\ 15\ 14}{\cancel{8}\cancel{6}\cancel{4}}$ $-\ 577$ $\overline{287}$ | Regroup from the hundreds place. Cross out 8 and write 7, and change 5 into 15. Then, subtract in the tens place: $15 - 7 = 8$, and the hundreds place: $7 - 5 = 2$. |

1.
$$672$$
$$-\ 384$$

2.
$$720$$
$$-\ 268$$

3.
$$937$$
$$-\ 241$$

4.
$$416$$
$$-\ 299$$

5.
$$802$$
$$-\ 574$$

6.
$$671$$
$$-\ 495$$

7.
$$592$$
$$-\ 347$$

8.
$$236$$
$$-\ 149$$

9.
$$955$$
$$-\ 266$$

10.
$$834$$
$$-\ 779$$

11.
$$330$$
$$-\ 182$$

12.
$$712$$
$$-\ 387$$

Trade First

With the **trade-first** method, you do the regrouping all at once. Put regrouped numbers over the "place."

	4	3	1
−	2	5	6

In the ones place, 6 cannot be subtracted from 1.

		2	11
	4	3̶	1̶
−	2	5	6

Trade 1 ten from the tens place for 10 ones, leaving 2 in the tens place and 11 in the ones place.

	3	12	11
	4̶	3̶	1̶
−	2	5	6

5 cannot be subtracted from 2, so trade 1 hundred from the hundreds place for 10 tens. This leaves a 3 in the hundreds place and 12 in the tens place.

	3	12	11
	4̶	3̶	1̶
−	2	5	6
	1	7	5

Then, subtract the numbers in every place to get the answer.

WRITE each difference using the trade-first method.

1.
```
  572
− 289
```

2.
```
  613
− 438
```

3.
```
  836
− 393
```

4.
```
  420
− 174
```

5.
```
  731
− 546
```

6.
```
  207
− 188
```

7.
```
  828
− 259
```

8.
```
  945
− 288
```

9.
```
  827
− 492
```

10.
```
  536
− 387
```

11.
```
  467
− 169
```

12.
```
  330
− 258
```

What's the Difference?

WRITE each difference.

HINT: Try using the methods of the last two pages, and decide which one works best for you.

1.
$$829 - 479$$

2.
$$740 - 272$$

3.
$$435 - 156$$

4.
$$942 - 766$$

5.
$$645 - 289$$

6.
$$511 - 388$$

7.
$$820 - 534$$

8.
$$717 - 619$$

9.
$$738 - 445$$

10.
$$927 - 490$$

11.
$$204 - 115$$

12.
$$625 - 356$$

13.
$$451 - 329$$

14.
$$872 - 185$$

15.
$$661 - 499$$

16.
$$500 - 139$$

It All Adds Up

WRITE each sum.

HINT: Add the columns starting in the ones place, the same way you would with two numbers.

Example:

```
   6 5              6 5              6 5
   2 7              2 7              2 7
 + 1 3            + 1 3            + 1 3
              5 + 7 + 3 = 15    5         1 + 6 + 2 + 1 = 10    1 0 5
```

1.
```
    7
    9
 +  4
```

2.
```
    6
    3
 +  8
```

3.
```
   12
    7
 +  6
```

4.
```
   35
    8
 +  7
```

5.
```
   46
   17
 +  6
```

6.
```
   90
   22
 + 73
```

7.
```
   56
   14
 + 66
```

8.
```
   41
   76
 + 26
```

9.
```
  187
   33
 + 29
```

10.
```
  432
   67
 + 14
```

11.
```
  520
  128
 + 73
```

12.
```
  426
  291
 + 83
```

13.
```
   76
   12
   58
 + 24
```

14.
```
   53
   68
   94
 + 11
```

15.
```
  208
  423
   50
 + 37
```

16.
```
  723
  109
   32
 + 95
```

Adding 3 or More Numbers

Pick Apart

WRITE each sum using partial sums.

```
          7 7 4
          1 2 8
        +   3 6
```

Add the numbers in the hundreds place.	700 + 100 =	8 0 0
Add the numbers in the tens place.	70 + 20 + 30 =	1 2 0
Add the numbers in the ones place.	4 + 8 + 6 =	+ 1 8
Then add the numbers together.		9 3 8

1.
```
    81
    23
  + 57
```

2.
```
   464
    39
  + 16
```

3.
```
   536
   182
  + 72
```

4.
```
   431
   208
  +325
```

5.
```
    64
    12
    45
  + 31
```

6.
```
   671
    53
    30
  + 19
```

7.
```
   325
   260
    18
  + 22
```

8.
```
   124
   505
   230
  + 11
```

It All Adds Up

WRITE each sum.

1.
```
  5,234
+    52
```

2.
```
  3,716
+    21
```

3.
```
  9,348
+    35
```

4.
```
  7,724
+    96
```

5.
```
  6,409
+   250
```

6.
```
  4,131
+   614
```

7.
```
  1,259
+   556
```

8.
```
  3,517
+   489
```

9.
```
  1,294
+ 1,603
```

10.
```
  3,371
+ 4,218
```

11.
```
  4,102
+ 1,451
```

12.
```
  4,525
+ 2,213
```

13.
```
  2,385
+ 3,836
```

14.
```
  1,680
+ 1,746
```

15.
```
  2,831
+ 1,282
```

16.
```
  8,057
+ 1,748
```

Adding & Subtracting 4-Digit Numbers

What's the Difference?

WRITE each difference.

1.
$$6,537 - 26$$

2.
$$1,398 - 72$$

3.
$$4,552 - 68$$

4.
$$5,117 - 44$$

5.
$$9,783 - 521$$

6.
$$7,468 - 154$$

7.
$$5,246 - 307$$

8.
$$2,287 - 295$$

9.
$$2,871 - 1,750$$

10.
$$8,599 - 3,129$$

11.
$$7,645 - 4,203$$

12.
$$9,328 - 5,211$$

13.
$$8,392 - 4,914$$

14.
$$5,042 - 2,263$$

15.
$$8,921 - 1,467$$

16.
$$6,490 - 3,581$$

Number Drop-off

Front-end estimation is a fast way to determine approximately how large a sum or difference will be.

For front-end estimation, make all but the leftmost digit of each number zero.

$$
\begin{array}{r} 6,658 \\ +\quad 217 \end{array}
\longrightarrow
\begin{array}{r} 6,000 \\ +\quad 200 \\ \hline 6,200 \end{array}
$$

6,658 becomes 6,000.
217 becomes 200.
6,000 + 200 = 6,200
6,658 + 217 = 6,875

ESTIMATE each sum using front-end estimation. Then WRITE the actual sum to see how close your estimate is to the sum.

1.
$$
\begin{array}{r} 423 \\ +\ 271 \\ \hline \end{array}
\qquad
\begin{array}{r} \\ +\ \underline{} \end{array}
$$

2.
$$
\begin{array}{r} 190 \\ +\ 724 \\ \hline \end{array}
\qquad
\begin{array}{r} \\ +\ \underline{} \end{array}
$$

3.
$$
\begin{array}{r} 2,385 \\ +\ 612 \\ \hline \end{array}
\qquad
\begin{array}{r} \\ +\ \underline{} \end{array}
$$

4.
$$
\begin{array}{r} 8,732 \\ +\ 958 \\ \hline \end{array}
\qquad
\begin{array}{r} \\ +\ \underline{} \end{array}
$$

5.
$$
\begin{array}{r} 3,361 \\ +4,518 \\ \hline \end{array}
\qquad
\begin{array}{r} \\ +\ \underline{} \end{array}
$$

6.
$$
\begin{array}{r} 2,112 \\ +1,308 \\ \hline \end{array}
\qquad
\begin{array}{r} \\ +\ \underline{} \end{array}
$$

Number Drop-off

ESTIMATE each difference using front-end estimation. Then WRITE the actual difference to see how close your estimate is to the difference.

For front-end estimation, make all but the leftmost digit of each number zero.

$$\begin{array}{r} 7,289 \\ -\ 351 \end{array} \longrightarrow \begin{array}{r} 7,000 \\ -\ 300 \\ \hline 6,700 \end{array}$$

7,289 becomes 7,000.
351 becomes 300.

7,000 – 300 = 6,700
7,289 – 351 = 6,938

1.
$$\begin{array}{r} 872 \\ -\ 661 \end{array}$$
$$-\ \underline{\qquad}$$

2.
$$\begin{array}{r} 925 \\ -\ 629 \end{array}$$
$$-\ \underline{\qquad}$$

3.
$$\begin{array}{r} 6,734 \\ -\ 322 \end{array}$$
$$-\ \underline{\qquad}$$

4.
$$\begin{array}{r} 1,283 \\ -\ 564 \end{array}$$
$$-\ \underline{\qquad}$$

5.
$$\begin{array}{r} 4,826 \\ -1,711 \end{array}$$
$$-\ \underline{\qquad}$$

6.
$$\begin{array}{r} 9,382 \\ -\ 7,449 \end{array}$$
$$-\ \underline{\qquad}$$

Round About

Rounding numbers before adding and subtracting them often produces a closer estimate than when using front-end estimation. ROUND to the nearest hundred, and ADD the numbers to find an estimate of each sum. WRITE the sum to see how close your estimate is to the sum.

$$
\begin{array}{r}
5,153 \\
+439 \\
\end{array}
\longrightarrow
\begin{array}{r}
5,200 \\
+400 \\
\hline
5,600
\end{array}
$$

5,153 rounded to the nearest hundred is 5,200.

439 rounded to the nearest hundred is 400.

5,200 + 400 = 5,600

5,153 + 439 = 5,592

1.
$$
\begin{array}{r}
436 \\
+251 \\
\hline
\end{array}
\qquad + \underline{\hspace{3em}}
$$

2.
$$
\begin{array}{r}
166 \\
+108 \\
\hline
\end{array}
\qquad + \underline{\hspace{3em}}
$$

3.
$$
\begin{array}{r}
3,524 \\
+367 \\
\hline
\end{array}
\qquad + \underline{\hspace{3em}}
$$

4.
$$
\begin{array}{r}
7,539 \\
+616 \\
\hline
\end{array}
\qquad + \underline{\hspace{3em}}
$$

5.
$$
\begin{array}{r}
2,345 \\
+2,354 \\
\hline
\end{array}
\qquad + \underline{\hspace{3em}}
$$

6.
$$
\begin{array}{r}
4,181 \\
+1,423 \\
\hline
\end{array}
\qquad + \underline{\hspace{3em}}
$$

Round About

ROUND to the nearest hundred, and SUBTRACT the numbers to find an estimate of each difference. WRITE the difference to see how close your estimate is to the difference.

$$
\begin{array}{r}
2,587 \\
-534 \\
\end{array}
\longrightarrow
\begin{array}{r}
2,600 \\
-500 \\
\hline
2,100 \\
\end{array}
$$

2,587 rounded to the nearest hundred is 2,600.
534 rounded to the nearest hundred is 500.

2,600 − 500 = 2,100
2,587 − 534 = 2,053

1.
$$
\begin{array}{r}
878 \\
-223 \\
\hline
\end{array}
$$
 − _____

2.
$$
\begin{array}{r}
795 \\
-519 \\
\hline
\end{array}
$$
 − _____

3.
$$
\begin{array}{r}
6,428 \\
-411 \\
\hline
\end{array}
$$
 − _____

4.
$$
\begin{array}{r}
4,493 \\
-897 \\
\hline
\end{array}
$$
 − _____

5.
$$
\begin{array}{r}
8,781 \\
-6,447 \\
\hline
\end{array}
$$
 − _____

6.
$$
\begin{array}{r}
7,064 \\
-1,815 \\
\hline
\end{array}
$$
 − _____

Work It Out

Alex loves to collect baseball cards. He has 523 cards in his collection, and he has plans to buy 25 more cards on the weekend.

1. How many baseball cards will Alex have? _____

Pop sensation Sara O'Hara just performed two spectacular concerts. On Friday, 3,814 tickets were sold. On Saturday, 4,990 tickets were sold.

2. How many total tickets were sold? _____

Alex and Jane had a lemonade stand for 4 hot days. On the first day, they sold 23 cups of lemonade. The next day, they sold 17 cups. The third day was the hottest, and they sold 42 cups. On the last day, they sold 25 cups.

3. How many total cups of lemonade did they sell? _____

Work It Out

Mike and Marissa are on an 875-mile road trip with their parents. In three days, they traveled 526 miles.

1. How many miles do they have

   left to go? _____

Springfield Elementary School collected 1,081 cans for two soup kitchens in town. They gave 458 cans to the first soup kitchen.

2. How many cans will they give to the other soup kitchen? _____

Hannah racked up the highest score on Starship Space Race with 7,129 points. Ricky has the second-highest score with 6,832 points.

3. How many points higher is Hannah's score than Ricky's? _____

Unit Rewind

WRITE each sum or difference.

1.
$$\begin{array}{r} 54 \\ +\ 21 \\ \hline \end{array}$$

2.
$$\begin{array}{r} 78 \\ +\ 33 \\ \hline \end{array}$$

3.
$$\begin{array}{r} 86 \\ -\ 64 \\ \hline \end{array}$$

4.
$$\begin{array}{r} 67 \\ -\ 28 \\ \hline \end{array}$$

5.
$$\begin{array}{r} 438 \\ +\ 240 \\ \hline \end{array}$$

6.
$$\begin{array}{r} 582 \\ +\ 349 \\ \hline \end{array}$$

7.
$$\begin{array}{r} 928 \\ -\ 623 \\ \hline \end{array}$$

8.
$$\begin{array}{r} 471 \\ -\ 177 \\ \hline \end{array}$$

9.
$$\begin{array}{r} 1,282 \\ +\ 512 \\ \hline \end{array}$$

10.
$$\begin{array}{r} 4,916 \\ +\ 684 \\ \hline \end{array}$$

11.
$$\begin{array}{r} 3,671 \\ -\ 610 \\ \hline \end{array}$$

12.
$$\begin{array}{r} 7,102 \\ -\ 493 \\ \hline \end{array}$$

13.
$$\begin{array}{r} 2,830 \\ +6,129 \\ \hline \end{array}$$

14.
$$\begin{array}{r} 3,817 \\ +3,195 \\ \hline \end{array}$$

15.
$$\begin{array}{r} 9,844 \\ -9,213 \\ \hline \end{array}$$

16.
$$\begin{array}{r} 4,164 \\ -2,837 \\ \hline \end{array}$$

Unit Rewind

First, ESTIMATE each problem using front-end estimation. Then ESTIMATE each problem by rounding to the nearest hundred. WRITE the sum or difference to compare your estimates.

	Front End	Rounding

1.
```
   531
+  324
```
+ _____   + _____

2.
```
  1,249
+   217
```
+ _____   + _____

3.
```
   352
-  144
```
− _____   − _____

4.
```
  4,671
-   728
```
− _____   − _____

Lunch Boxes

WRITE the total number of food items you see in the four lunch boxes.

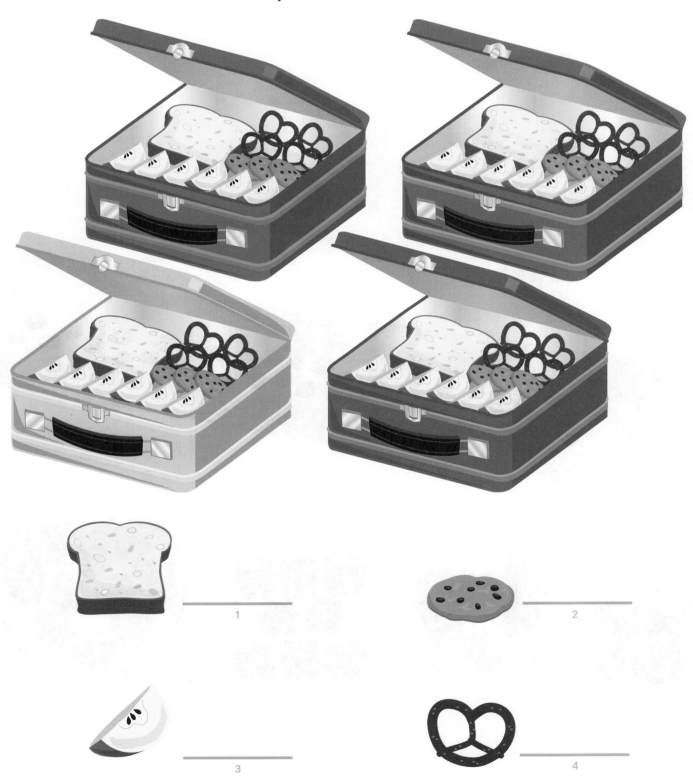

1 _____

2 _____

3 _____

4 _____

Pick a Package

How many of each type of box would be needed to pack the chocolates on the conveyor belt? WRITE the answer below each box.

1 _____

2 _____

3 _____

4 _____

Get in Line

SKIP COUNT and WRITE the missing numbers.

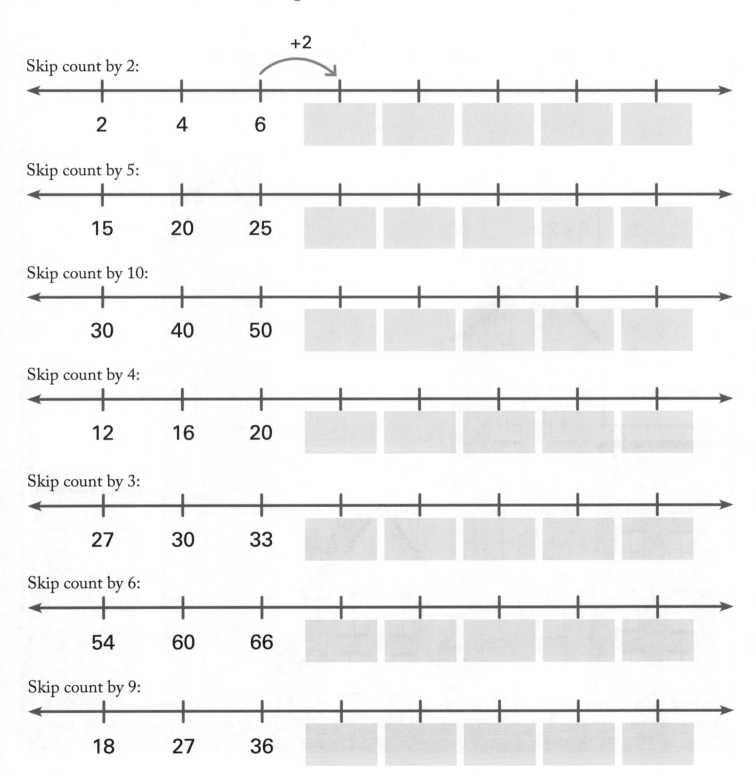

Skip count by 2:

+2

2   4   6

Skip count by 5:

15   20   25

Skip count by 10:

30   40   50

Skip count by 4:

12   16   20

Skip count by 3:

27   30   33

Skip count by 6:

54   60   66

Skip count by 9:

18   27   36

Buildings Times Two

WRITE the number of windows you see on each building on the sign above the building.

Picture It

Use the pictures to help you answer each problem. WRITE the answer for each set of pictures.

$5 \times 3 =$ _____
1

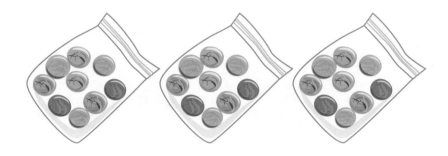

$9 \times 3 =$ _____
2

$7 \times 3 =$ _____
3

$6 \times 4 =$ _____
4

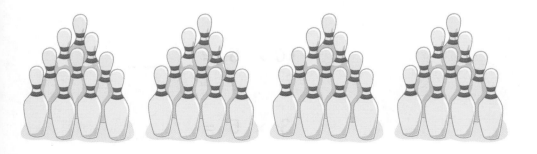

$10 \times 4 =$ _____
5

High Fives

Use the pictures to help you answer each problem. WRITE the answer to each problem.

HINT: Think of each problem as counting the total number of fingers on a number of hands.

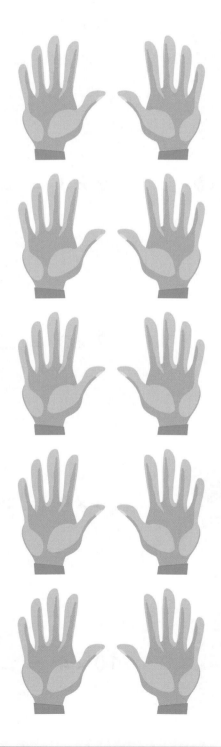

$4 \times 5 =$ ___20___

1

$1 \times 5 =$ _____

2

$7 \times 5 =$ _____

3

$6 \times 5 =$ _____

4

$2 \times 5 =$ _____

5

$9 \times 5 =$ _____

6

$5 \times 5 =$ _____

7

$8 \times 5 =$ _____

8

$10 \times 5 =$ _____

9

$3 \times 5 =$ _____

10

Magic Tricks

Multiplying any number by 1 gives you the same number.

Each hat has 1 rabbit.
3 hats have 3 rabbits.
$3 \times 1 = 3$

Multiplying any number by 0 gives you 0.

Each hat has 0 rabbits.
3 hats have 0 rabbits.
$3 \times 0 = 0$

WRITE the answer to each problem.

1.	2.	3.	4.	5.	6.
6	7	3	2	10	8
× 1	× 0	× 1	× 0	× 1	× 0

7.	8.	9.	10.	11.	12.
5	4	1	5	9	10
× 1	× 0	× 1	× 0	× 1	× 0

13.	14.	15.	16.	17.	18.
7	6	8	1	2	9
× 1	× 0	× 1	× 0	× 1	× 0

Picture It

Use the pictures to help you answer each problem. WRITE the answer for each set of pictures.

1.

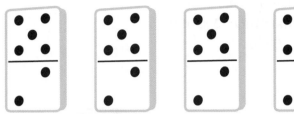

$7 \times 4 =$ _____

2.

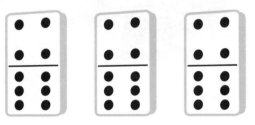

$10 \times 3 =$ _____

3.

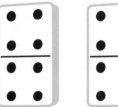 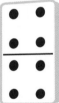   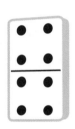 

$8 \times 6 =$ _____

4.

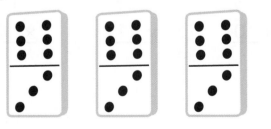

$9 \times 4 =$ _____

5.

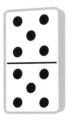 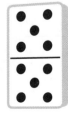 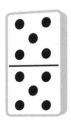  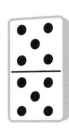 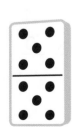

$10 \times 6 =$ _____

Computation Station

A **product** is the number you get when you multiply two numbers together. A **factor** is one of the numbers being multiplied.

Example:

    6   factor
  × 7   factor
  4 2   product

factor

factor →

×	0	1	2	3	4	5	6	7	8	9	10
0	0	0	0	0	0	0	0	0	0	0	0
1	0	1	2	3	4	5	6	7	8	9	10
2	0	2	4	6	8	10	12	14	16	18	20
3	0	3	6	9	12	15	18	21	24	27	30
4	0	4	8	12	16	20	24	28	32	36	40
5	0	5	10	15	20	25	30	35	40	45	50
6	0	6	12	18	24	30	36	42	48	54	60
7	0	7	14	21	28	35	42	49	56	63	70
8	0	8	16	24	32	40	48	56	64	72	80
9	0	9	18	27	36	45	54	63	72	81	90
10	0	10	20	30	40	50	60	70	80	90	100

LOCATE each factor in the multiplication table. The square where the row and column meet shows you the product. WRITE each product.

1.
   2
× 5

2.
   8
× 4

3.
  10
×10

4.
   3
× 9

5.
   5
× 7

6.
   6
× 1

7.
  10
× 3

8.
   0
× 7

9.
   4
× 3

10.
   7
× 7

11.
   9
× 6

12.
   5
× 5

13.
   8
× 2

14.
   4
× 9

15.
   3
× 7

16.
   9
× 0

17.
   8
× 8

18.
   2
× 1

Computation Station

WRITE each product.

1. $4 \times 1 =$ _____

2. $7 \times 5 =$ _____

3. $8 \times 3 =$ _____

4. $6 \times 2 =$ _____

5. $9 \times 5 =$ _____

6. $10 \times 2 =$ _____

7. $6 \times 6 =$ _____

8. $1 \times 0 =$ _____

9. $1 \times 8 =$ _____

10. $9 \times 9 =$ _____

11. $7 \times 4 =$ _____

12. $5 \times 3 =$ _____

13.
$$\begin{array}{r} 10 \\ \times\ 8 \\ \hline \end{array}$$

14.
$$\begin{array}{r} 0 \\ \times\ 2 \\ \hline \end{array}$$

15.
$$\begin{array}{r} 9 \\ \times\ 4 \\ \hline \end{array}$$

16.
$$\begin{array}{r} 5 \\ \times\ 6 \\ \hline \end{array}$$

17.
$$\begin{array}{r} 8 \\ \times\ 2 \\ \hline \end{array}$$

18.
$$\begin{array}{r} 4 \\ \times\ 4 \\ \hline \end{array}$$

19.
$$\begin{array}{r} 7 \\ \times\ 3 \\ \hline \end{array}$$

20.
$$\begin{array}{r} 9 \\ \times\ 8 \\ \hline \end{array}$$

21.
$$\begin{array}{r} 4 \\ \times\ 2 \\ \hline \end{array}$$

22.
$$\begin{array}{r} 1 \\ \times\ 1 \\ \hline \end{array}$$

23.
$$\begin{array}{r} 6 \\ \times\ 3 \\ \hline \end{array}$$

24.
$$\begin{array}{r} 9 \\ \times\ 5 \\ \hline \end{array}$$

25.
$$\begin{array}{r} 4 \\ \times\ 5 \\ \hline \end{array}$$

26.
$$\begin{array}{r} 10 \\ \times\ 4 \\ \hline \end{array}$$

27.
$$\begin{array}{r} 0 \\ \times\ 0 \\ \hline \end{array}$$

28.
$$\begin{array}{r} 2 \\ \times\ 9 \\ \hline \end{array}$$

29.
$$\begin{array}{r} 5 \\ \times 10 \\ \hline \end{array}$$

30.
$$\begin{array}{r} 3 \\ \times\ 3 \\ \hline \end{array}$$

Fair Share

The twins aren't happy unless they get the same number of everything. How many of each toy will they each get? WRITE the answers.

1. _____ cars

2. _____ marbles

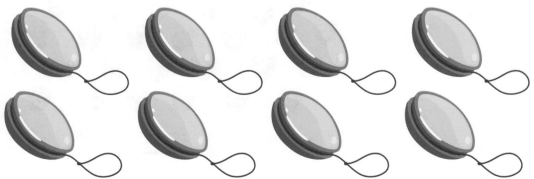

3. _____ yo-yos

Fair Share

WRITE the number of gems each pirate will get if they split the treasure equally.

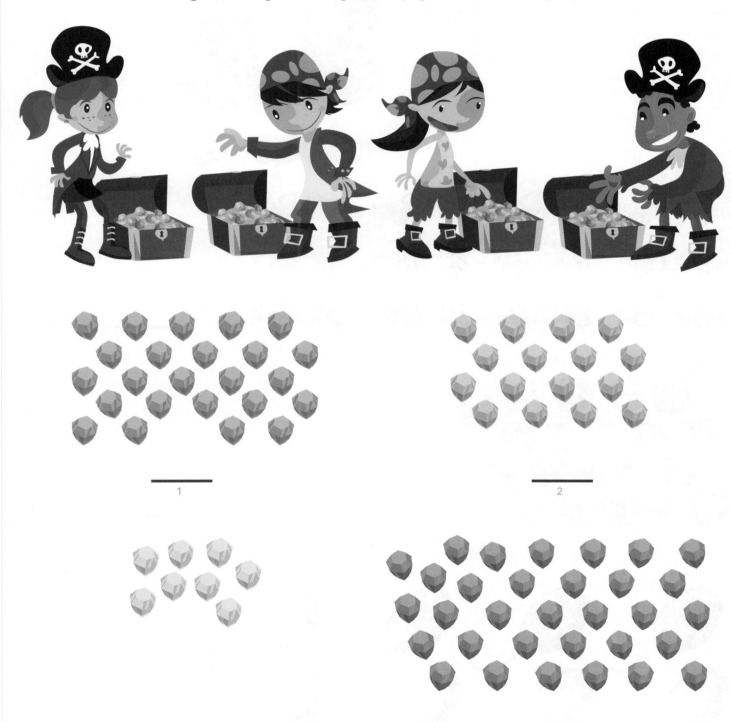

1 _____

2 _____

3 _____

4 _____

Bugged Out

CIRCLE groups of three bugs. WRITE the number of groups in each set.

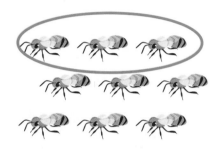

$9 \div 3 =$ _____
₁

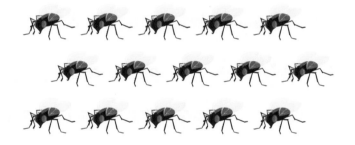

$15 \div 3 =$ _____
₂

$27 \div 3 =$ _____
₃

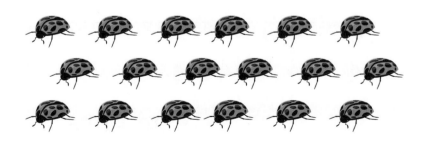

$18 \div 3 =$ _____
₄

Iced Over

Use the pictures to help you answer each problem. WRITE the answers.

HINT: Count the number of ice cubes in each group.

$18 \div 3 =$ _____
₁

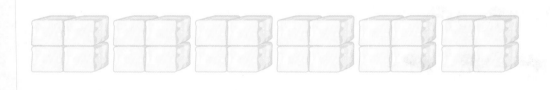

$24 \div 6 =$ _____
₂

$25 \div 5 =$ _____
₃

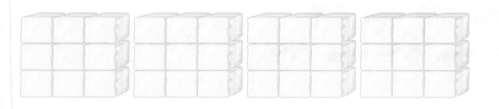

$36 \div 4 =$ _____
₄

$20 \div 10 =$ _____
₅

Computation Station

A **quotient** is the number you get when you divide one number by another number. You divide the **dividend** by the **divisor**.

Example:

$$\text{divisor } 3 \overline{)18} \quad \begin{array}{l} 6 \quad \text{quotient} \\ 18 \quad \text{dividend} \end{array}$$

×	0	1	2	3	4	5	6	7	8	9	10
0	0	0	0	0	0	0	0	0	0	0	0
1	0	1	2	3	4	5	6	7	8	9	10
2	0	2	4	6	8	10	12	14	16	18	20
3	0	3	6	9	12	15	18	21	24	27	30
4	0	4	8	12	16	20	24	28	32	36	40
5	0	5	10	15	20	25	30	35	40	45	50
6	0	6	12	18	24	30	36	42	48	54	60
7	0	7	14	21	28	35	42	49	56	63	70
8	0	8	16	24	32	40	48	56	64	72	80
9	0	9	18	27	36	45	54	63	72	81	90
10	0	10	20	30	40	50	60	70	80	90	100

WRITE each quotient.

1. $2\overline{)16}$

2. $8\overline{)24}$

3. $9\overline{)90}$

4. $1\overline{)7}$

5. $3\overline{)21}$

6. $7\overline{)14}$

7. $5\overline{)35}$

8. $7\overline{)56}$

9. $4\overline{)32}$

10. $8\overline{)48}$

11. $9\overline{)81}$

12. $2\overline{)12}$

13. $7\overline{)63}$

14. $1\overline{)3}$

15. $10\overline{)70}$

16. $3\overline{)9}$

17. $9\overline{)36}$

18. $4\overline{)40}$

Dividing

Computation Station

WRITE each quotient.

1. $20 \div 5 =$ _____   2. $80 \div 8 =$ _____   3. $12 \div 6 =$ _____

4. $18 \div 2 =$ _____   5. $24 \div 3 =$ _____   6. $30 \div 6 =$ _____

7. $90 \div 10 =$ _____   8. $56 \div 8 =$ _____   9. $36 \div 6 =$ _____

10. $45 \div 5 =$ _____   11. $16 \div 4 =$ _____   12. $3 \div 1 =$ _____

13. $5 \overline{)15}$ 14. $5 \overline{)25}$ 15. $6 \overline{)24}$ 16. $10 \overline{)60}$ 17. $9 \overline{)72}$ 18. $1 \overline{)8}$

19. $2 \overline{)6}$ 20. $4 \overline{)40}$ 21. $7 \overline{)63}$ 22. $4 \overline{)28}$ 23. $3 \overline{)27}$ 24. $7 \overline{)49}$

25. $6 \overline{)54}$ 26. $7 \overline{)14}$ 27. $3 \overline{)30}$ 28. $9 \overline{)45}$ 29. $6 \overline{)48}$ 30. $5 \overline{)20}$

Factor Hunt

WRITE all of the factors of each number. Use the multiplication table to help you.

HINT: Write down all of the numbers that can be used to divide each number evenly. Remember that every number can be divided by itself and 1.

Example:

10 | 1 | 2 | 5 | 10 |

×	0	1	2	3	4	5	6	7	8	9	10
0	0	0	0	0	0	0	0	0	0	0	0
1	0	1	2	3	4	5	6	7	8	9	10
2	0	2	4	6	8	10	12	14	16	18	20
3	0	3	6	9	12	15	18	21	24	27	30
4	0	4	8	12	16	20	24	28	32	36	40
5	0	5	10	15	20	25	30	35	40	45	50
6	0	6	12	18	24	30	36	42	48	54	60
7	0	7	14	21	28	35	42	49	56	63	70
8	0	8	16	24	32	40	48	56	64	72	80
9	0	9	18	27	36	45	54	63	72	81	90
10	0	10	20	30	40	50	60	70	80	90	100

1. 4   

2. 6   

3. 9   

4. 12   

5. 15   

6. 16   

7. 18

Tic-Tac-Toe

A **multiple** is a number that can be divided evenly by another number. CIRCLE any number that is a multiple of the blue number. PUT an X through any number that is not a multiple. DRAW a line when you find three multiples in a row. The line can go across, down, or diagonally.

Example:

5

42	10	24
16	35	40
25	5	81

5

42	10	24
16	35	40
25	5	81

Multiples of 5 are
5, 10, 15, 20, 25,
30, 35, 40, 45, 50.

2

12	18	16
4	7	9
3	15	20

10

55	20	49
70	36	72
50	80	30

6

40	14	12
25	54	36
63	8	18

8

56	36	24
27	80	64
48	34	30

Work It Out

Each Roaring Racetrack set comes with 10 straight tracks, 8 curved tracks, 3 track loops, and 4 cars.

1. How many pieces are in 5 Roaring Racetrack sets?

   Straight tracks _____

   Curved tracks _____

   Track loops _____

   Cars _____

ROARING RACETRACK

Jonah invited 6 friends over for hot dogs. Each of his friends can eat 3 hot dogs.

2. How many hot dogs does Jonah need to make? _____

Work It Out

Felix bought a box of 36 dog biscuits and 12 cans of dog food for his 6 dogs.

1. If each dog gets the same amount, how much food will each dog get?

   _____ dog biscuits

   _____ cans of food

Zoë has 64 stickers and a sticker album with 8 pages.

2. If she puts the same number of stickers on each page, how many stickers

   will be on 1 page? _____

Computation Station

WRITE each product.

1.	2.	3.	4.	5.	6.
3	9	6	5	7	10
× 5	× 8	× 4	× 1	× 0	× 2

7.	8.	9.	10.	11.	12.
8	3	5	2	7	4
× 8	× 3	× 9	× 8	× 9	× 7

13.	14.	15.	16.	17.	18.
9	10	0	6	9	6
× 4	× 6	× 9	× 8	× 9	× 3

WRITE each quotient.

19.	20.	21.	22.	23.	24.
5)20	7)42	3)15	10)70	9)9	6)12

25.	26.	27.	28.	29.	30.
2)18	8)56	9)90	7)21	6)36	4)12

31.	32.	33.	34.	35.	36.
5)25	4)8	7)28	4)32	9)27	5)35

Fact Finder

WRITE all of the multiplication and division number sentences that go with each picture.

Example:

3 rows of 4 jellybeans = 12 total jellybeans

3	×	4	=	12
4	×	3	=	12
12	÷	3	=	4
12	÷	4	=	3

1.

_____ × _____ = _____

_____ × _____ = _____

_____ ÷ _____ = _____

_____ ÷ _____ = _____

2.

_____ × _____ = _____

_____ × _____ = _____

_____ ÷ _____ = _____

_____ ÷ _____ = _____

3.

_____ × _____ = _____

_____ × _____ = _____

_____ ÷ _____ = _____

_____ ÷ _____ = _____

4.

_____ × _____ = _____

_____ × _____ = _____

_____ ÷ _____ = _____

_____ ÷ _____ = _____

Any Way You Slice It

WRITE the fraction for each picture.

Example:

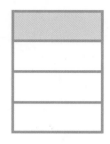

$\dfrac{1}{4}$ ← the number of shaded sections
← the total number of sections

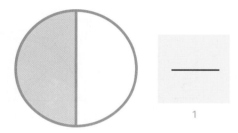

1 ____

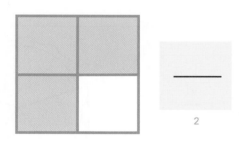

2 ____

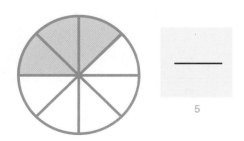

3 ____

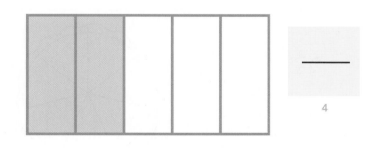

4 ____

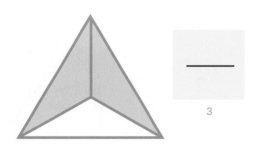

5 ____

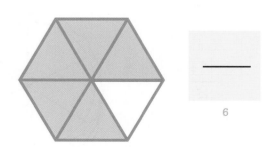

6 ____

Piece of Cake

COLOR the cake pieces to match each fraction.

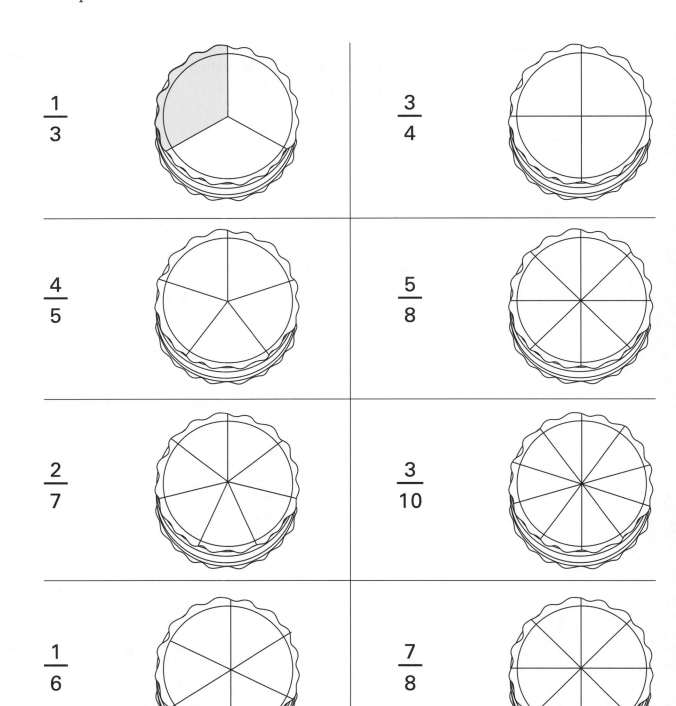

$$\frac{1}{3}$$

$$\frac{3}{4}$$

$$\frac{4}{5}$$

$$\frac{5}{8}$$

$$\frac{2}{7}$$

$$\frac{3}{10}$$

$$\frac{1}{6}$$

$$\frac{7}{8}$$

Fraction Bars

WRITE the fraction for each picture.

1. _____

2. _____

3. _____

4. _____

5. _____

6. _____

7. _____

8. _____

Parts of a Whole

Odd One Out

CROSS OUT the picture or fraction in each row that does **not** match the others.

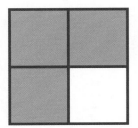 $\dfrac{3}{4}$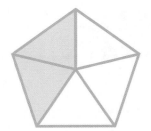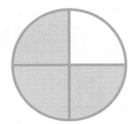

$\dfrac{5}{6}$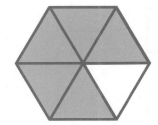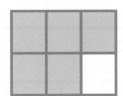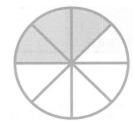

   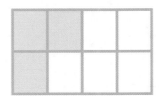    $\dfrac{3}{8}$

   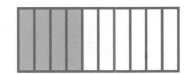 $\dfrac{4}{9}$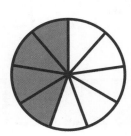

Shaded Shapes

WRITE the fraction for each set.

Example: $\dfrac{5}{6}$ ← the number of shaded circles
← the total number of circles

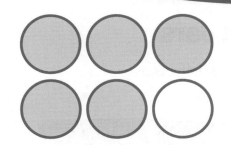

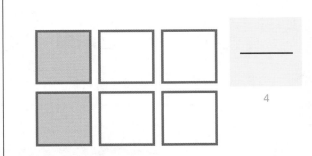

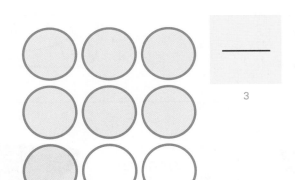

1

2

3

4

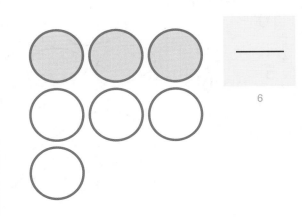

5

6

Jellybean Jars

COLOR each jar of jellybeans.

$\dfrac{3}{7}$ green

$\dfrac{4}{7}$ blue

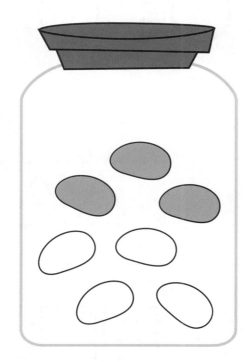

$\dfrac{1}{8}$ purple

$\dfrac{2}{8}$ green

$\dfrac{5}{8}$ orange

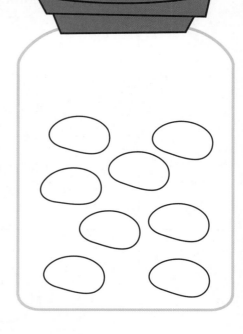

$\dfrac{2}{10}$ red

$\dfrac{3}{10}$ yellow

$\dfrac{5}{10}$ purple

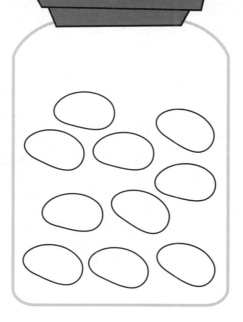

$\dfrac{1}{9}$ orange

$\dfrac{2}{9}$ red

$\dfrac{3}{9}$ blue

$\dfrac{3}{9}$ purple

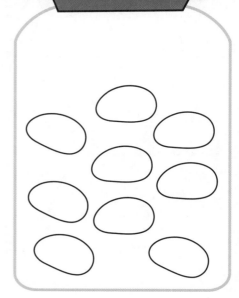

Fashion Fractions

WRITE the fraction for each description.

1. Fraction of kids wearing orange shirts $\dfrac{3}{7}$

2. Fraction of kids wearing hats ——

3. Fraction of girls wearing skirts ——

4. Fraction of boys wearing sunglasses ——

5. Fraction of girls with red hair ——

6. Fraction of boys wearing shorts ——

Find the Same

CIRCLE the picture in each row that matches the fraction.

$\dfrac{4}{5}$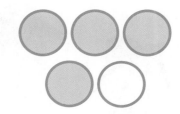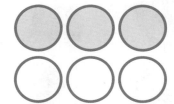

$\dfrac{7}{9}$

$\dfrac{1}{6}$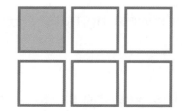

$\dfrac{3}{10}$

Piece of Cake

COLOR the cake pieces to match each fraction. Then CIRCLE the larger fraction.

HINT: The larger fraction is the one with more cake colored.

$\dfrac{1}{6}$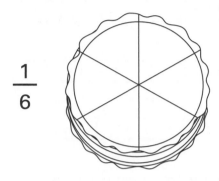

$\dfrac{1}{5}$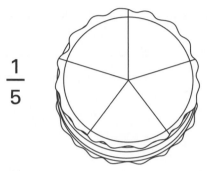

$\dfrac{4}{7}$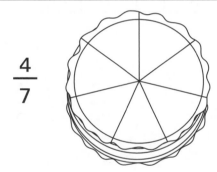

$\dfrac{3}{8}$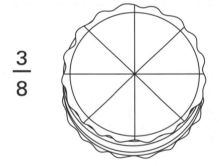

$\dfrac{1}{4}$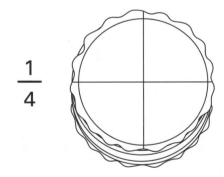

$\dfrac{2}{9}$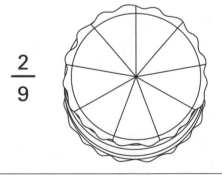

$\dfrac{7}{10}$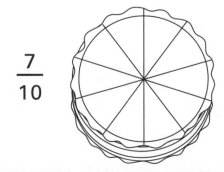

$\dfrac{7}{8}$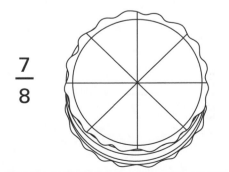

Matched or Mismatched?

WRITE >, <, or = in each box.

HINT: Use the fraction bars to help you picture the fractions.

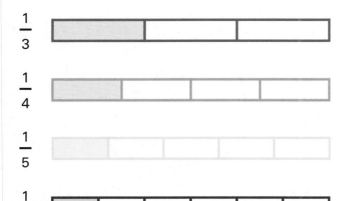

$\dfrac{1}{3}$

$\dfrac{1}{4}$

$\dfrac{1}{5}$

$\dfrac{1}{6}$

$\dfrac{1}{7}$

$\dfrac{1}{8}$

$\dfrac{1}{9}$

$\dfrac{1}{10}$

$\dfrac{2}{5}$ ☐ $\dfrac{1}{4}$
1

$\dfrac{5}{6}$ ☐ $\dfrac{1}{3}$
2

$\dfrac{1}{6}$ ☐ $\dfrac{4}{9}$
3

$\dfrac{4}{8}$ ☐ $\dfrac{5}{10}$
4

$\dfrac{7}{10}$ ☐ $\dfrac{7}{8}$
5

$\dfrac{4}{4}$ ☐ $\dfrac{5}{8}$
6

$\dfrac{5}{9}$ ☐ $\dfrac{6}{9}$
7

$\dfrac{2}{7}$ ☐ $\dfrac{2}{4}$
8

$\dfrac{5}{9}$ ☐ $\dfrac{4}{10}$
9

$\dfrac{3}{6}$ ☐ $\dfrac{3}{7}$
10

$\dfrac{5}{7}$ ☐ $\dfrac{5}{8}$
11

$\dfrac{7}{7}$ ☐ $\dfrac{9}{9}$
12

Match Up

WRITE the number next to each fraction. Then DRAW lines to match fractions that are the same.

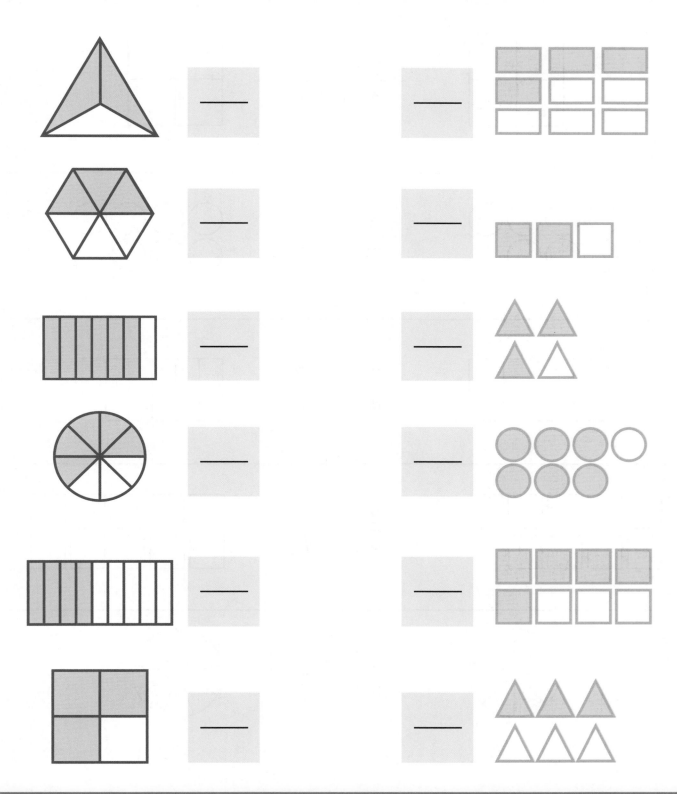

Matched or Mismatched?

COLOR the pictures to match each fraction. Then WRITE >, <, or = in each box.

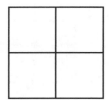 $\dfrac{3}{4}$ $\boxed{}$ $\dfrac{2}{4}$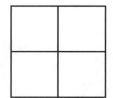

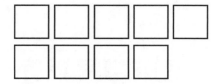 $\dfrac{3}{7}$ $\boxed{}$ $\dfrac{5}{7}$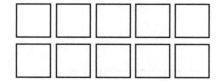

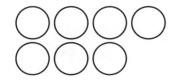 $\dfrac{2}{4}$ $\boxed{}$ $\dfrac{3}{6}$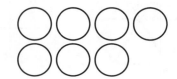

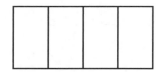 $\dfrac{3}{9}$ $\boxed{}$ $\dfrac{7}{10}$

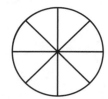 $\dfrac{5}{8}$ $\boxed{}$ $\dfrac{5}{9}$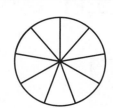

Length

Measure Up

WRITE the approximate length of each object in inches (in.) and centimeters (cm).

1. about _____ in.   about _____ cm

2. about _____ in.   about _____ cm

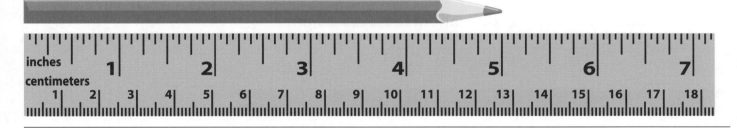

3. about _____ in.   about _____ cm

4. about _____ in.   about _____ cm

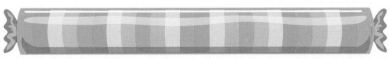

Rulers Rule

MEASURE each piece of ribbon with a ruler. WRITE the approximate length of each object in inches (in.) and centimeters (cm).

1.

about _____ in.   about _____ cm

2.

about _____ in.   about _____ cm

3.

about _____ in.   about _____ cm

4.

about _____ in.   about _____ cm

5.

about _____ in.   about _____ cm

6.

about _____ in.   about _____ cm

Preferred Measure

Which unit of measure would you use to measure each object? CIRCLE *inch*, *foot*, or *yard*.

NOTE: These rulers show how the units compare to each other. They are not actual size.

inch

foot

yard

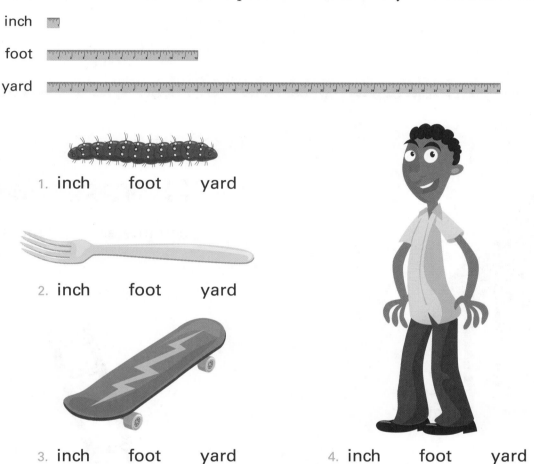

1. inch   foot   yard

2. inch   foot   yard

3. inch   foot   yard

4. inch   foot   yard

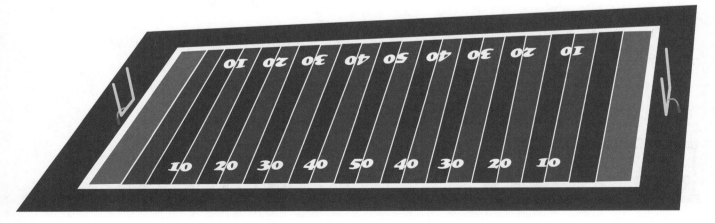

5. inch   foot   yard

Which Is Best?

Which is the best unit to measure the length of each object? CIRCLE *centimeter* or *meter*.

NOTE: These rulers show how the units compare to each other. They are not actual size.

centimeter

meter

2. centimeter   meter

3. centimeter   meter

5. centimeter   meter

1. centimeter   meter

4. centimeter   meter

6. centimeter   meter

Match Up

DRAW lines to match the pictures with equal amounts of liquid volume.

Example:

2 cups = 1 pint   2 pints = 1 quart   4 quarts = 1 gallon

Which Is Best?

Which is the best unit to measure the liquid volume of each object? CIRCLE *cup*, *pint*, *quart*, or *gallon*.

1. cup   pint   quart   gallon

2. cup   pint   quart   gallon

3. cup   pint   quart   gallon

4. cup   pint   quart   gallon

5. cup   pint   quart   gallon

6. cup   pint   quart   gallon

7. cup   pint   quart   gallon

8. cup   pint   quart   gallon

Circle the Same

CIRCLE any item that can hold at least 1 liter of liquid.

Example:

1 liter (1 L)
1 liter = 1,000 milliliters

120 milliliters (120 mL)

Which Is Best?

Which is the best unit to measure the liquid volume of each object? CIRCLE *milliliter* or *liter*.

1.   milliliter   liter

2.   milliliter   liter

3.   milliliter   liter

4.   milliliter   liter

5.   milliliter   liter

6.   milliliter   liter

7.   milliliter   liter

8.   milliliter   liter

Circle It

CIRCLE any item that weighs less than 1 pound.

Example:

1 pound (1 lb)
1 pound = 16 ounces

1 ounce (1 oz)

Weight

Which Is Best?

Which is the best unit to measure the weight of each object? CIRCLE *ounce* or *pound*.

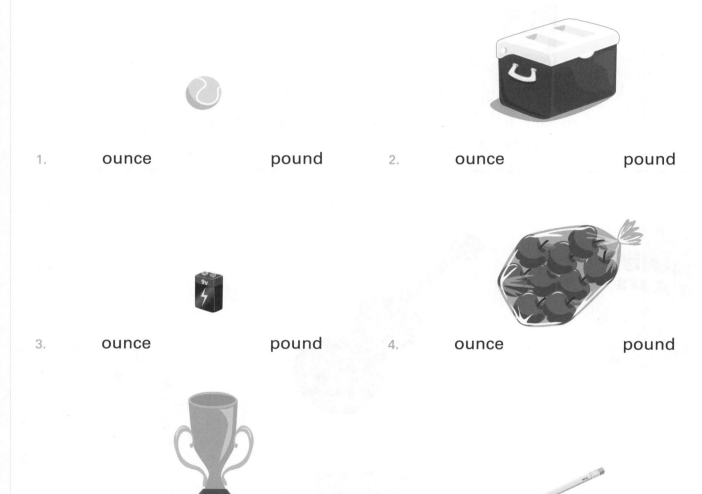

1.   ounce   pound   2.   ounce   pound

3.   ounce   pound   4.   ounce   pound

5.   ounce   pound   6.   ounce   pound

7.   ounce   pound   8.   ounce   pound

Circle It

CIRCLE any item that weighs more than 1 kilogram.

Example:

1 kilogram (1 kg)
1 kilogram = 1,000 grams

1 gram (1 g)

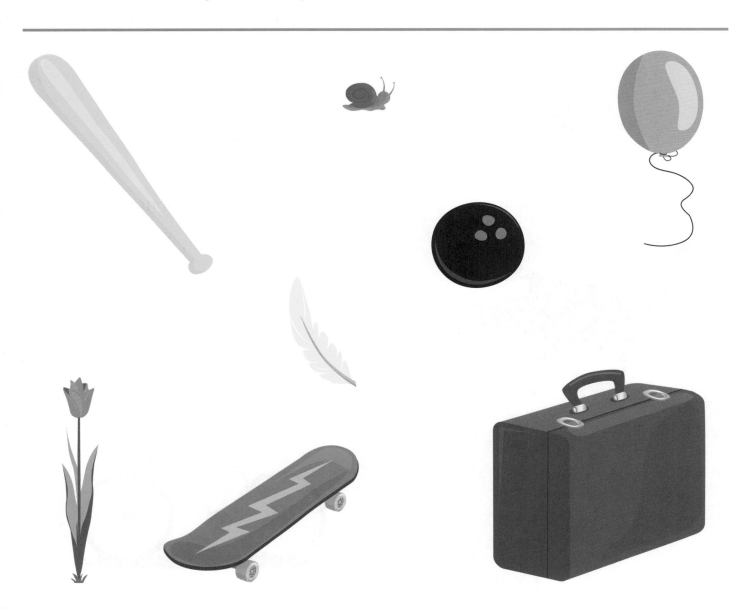

Which Is Best?

Which is the best unit to measure the weight of each object? CIRCLE *gram* or *kilogram*.

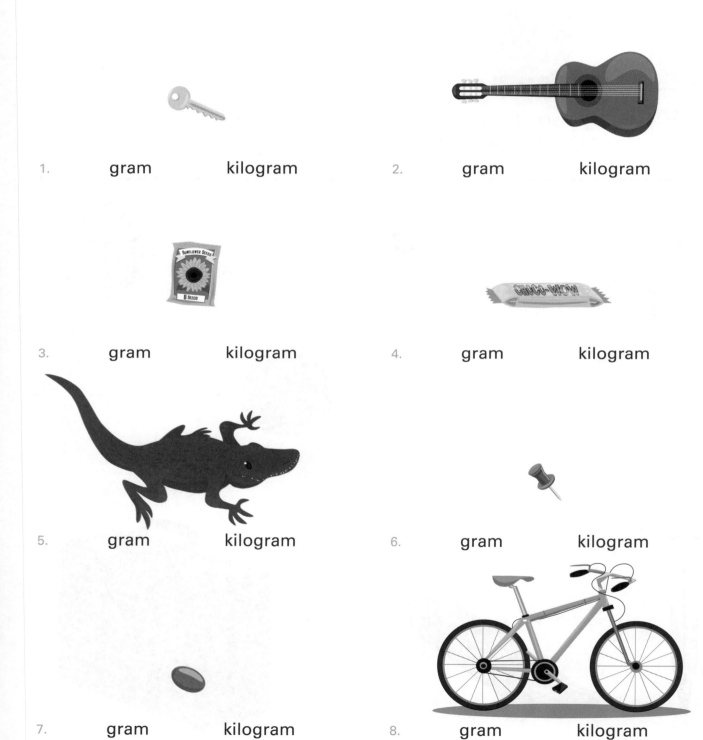

1. gram   kilogram

2. gram   kilogram

3. gram   kilogram

4. gram   kilogram

5. gram   kilogram

6. gram   kilogram

7. gram   kilogram

8. gram   kilogram

Measure Up

MEASURE each temperature to the nearest degree. WRITE the temperature in degrees Fahrenheit (°F) and degrees Celsius (°C).

Example:

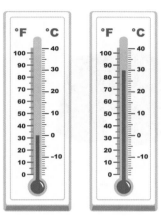

Water freezes at 32°F or 0°C.
A hot summer day might be 86°F or 30°C.

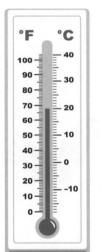

1. _____ °F

_____ °C

2. _____ °F

_____ °C

3. _____ °F

_____ °C

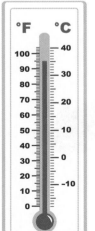

4. _____ °F

_____ °C

5. _____ °F

_____ °C

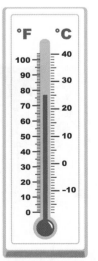

6. _____ °F

_____ °C

Circle It

CIRCLE the appropriate item of clothing for the weather shown on each thermometer.

Rulers Rule

WRITE the approximate length of each worm in inches (in.) and centimeters (cm).

1. about _____ in.   about _____ cm

2. about _____ in.   about _____ cm

3. about _____ in.   about _____ cm

4. about _____ in.   about _____ cm

Measuring Mash-up

CIRCLE the best unit of measure for each object.

1.   ounce   pound

2.   gallon   pint

3.   gram   kilogram

4.   yard   inch

5.   quart   cup

6.   pint   gallon

7.   liter   milliliter

8.   centimeter   meter

Matched or Mismatched?

WRITE >, <, or = in each box.

1 centimeter ☐ 1 meter   1 gallon ☐ 1 pint

1 kilogram ☐ 1,000 grams   1 yard ☐ 1 foot

2 pints ☐ 1 quart   15 ounces ☐ 1 pound

1 yard ☐ 6 inches   50 milliliters ☐ 1 liter

3,000 grams ☐ 1 kilogram   1 foot ☐ 12 inches

5 cups ☐ 3 pints   6 quarts ☐ 1 gallon

Measuring Mash-up

CIRCLE the best unit of measure for each object.

1. **Length of a speedboat**   centimeter   meter   inch

2. **Body temperature**   gram   milliliter   degrees

3. **Weight of a caterpillar**   pound   yard   gram

4. **Volume of a drinking glass**   cup   gallon   kilogram

5. **Weight of a baby**   gram   pound   quart

6. **Length of a toe**   centimeter   foot   meter

7. **Volume of a washing machine**   milliliter   gallon   cup

8. **Length of a shoelace**   yard   meter   inch

Matched Set

COLOR all of the shapes in each row that match the word.

HINT: A square is a special type of rectangle.

circle

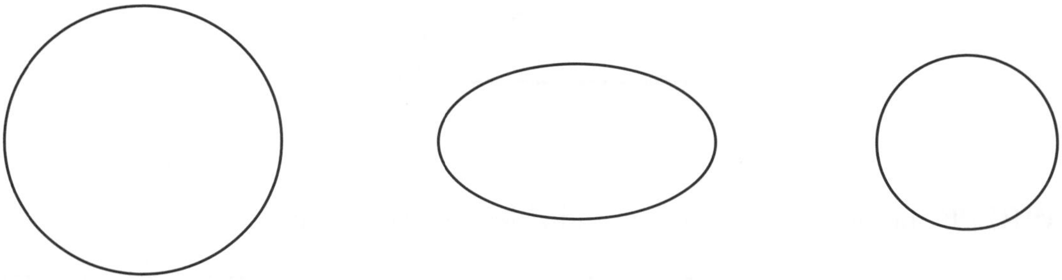

square

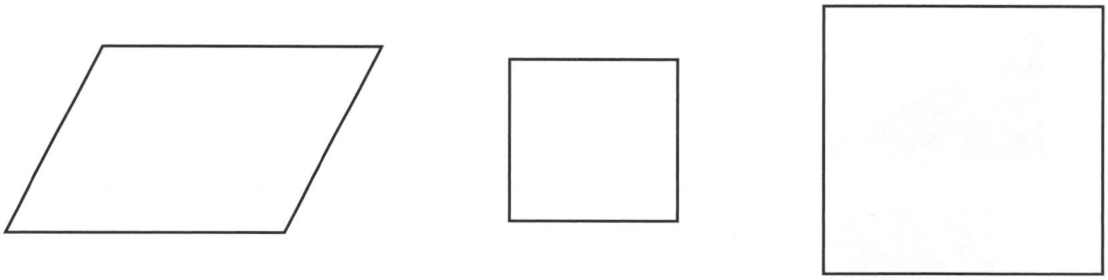

triangle

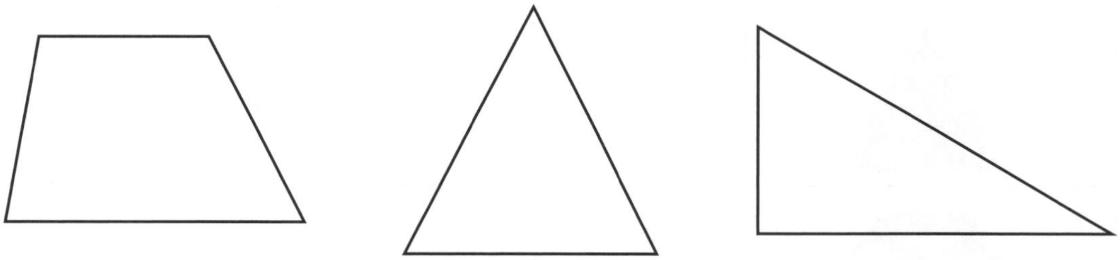

rectangle

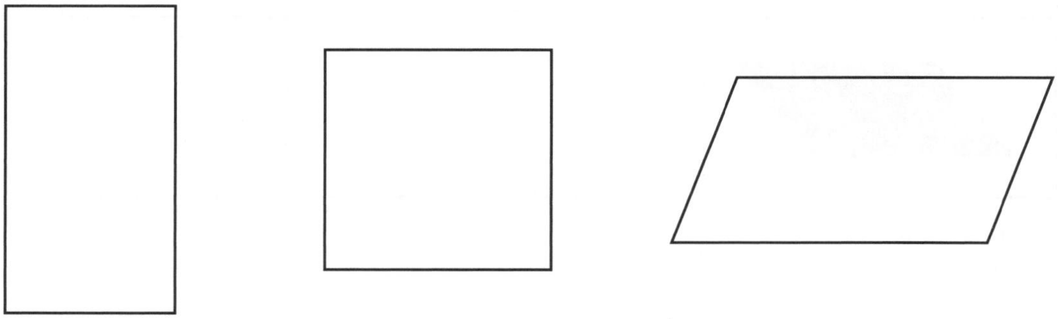

Shape Up

A **vertex** is where two lines meet. A **side** is the line between two vertices.

Example:

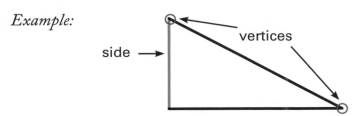

side →

vertices

WRITE the number of vertices and sides for each shape.

	Number of Vertices	Number of Sides

Around We Go

Perimeter is the distance around a two-dimensional shape. To find the perimeter, add all of the side lengths. For shapes with sides that are all the same length, multiply the length of one side by the number of sides.

Example:

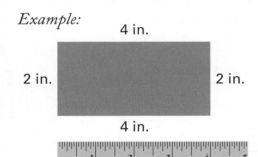

4 in.

2 in.   2 in.

4 in.

4 + 2 + 4 + 2 = 12
The perimeter of this rectangle is 12 in.

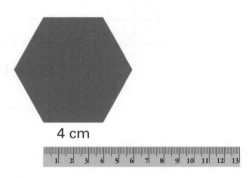

4 cm

4 x 6 = 24
The perimeter of this hexagon is 24 cm.

WRITE the perimeter of each shape.

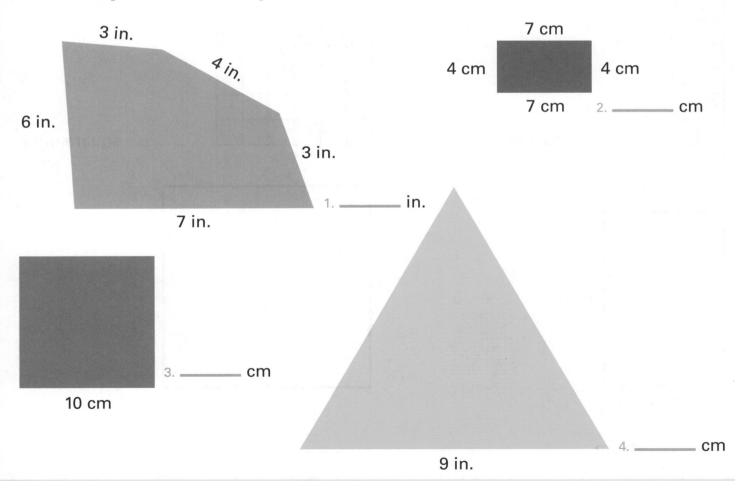

3 in.

4 in.

6 in.

3 in.

7 in.

1. _____ in.

7 cm

4 cm   4 cm

7 cm

2. _____ cm

10 cm

3. _____ cm

9 in.

4. _____ cm

Plane Shapes

Squared Away

Area is the size of the surface of a shape, and it is measured in square units. WRITE the area of each shape.

Example: 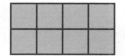 To find the area, multiply the height by the width. This rectangle is 2 square units high by 4 square units wide. 2 x 4 = 8.

1 square unit

The area of this rectangle is 8 square units.

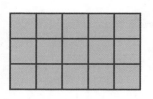

1. _____ square units

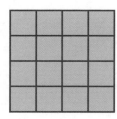

2. _____ square units

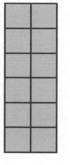

3. _____ square units

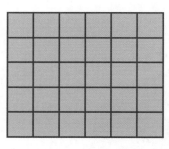

4. _____ square units

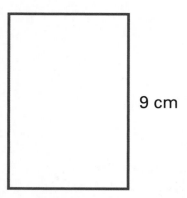

9 cm

6 cm

5. _____ sq cm

5 in.

6. _____ sq in.

Find the Same

CIRCLE the object in each row that is the same shape as the first shape.

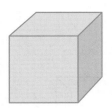   

Odd One Out

CROSS OUT the shape in each row that is **not** the same as the others.

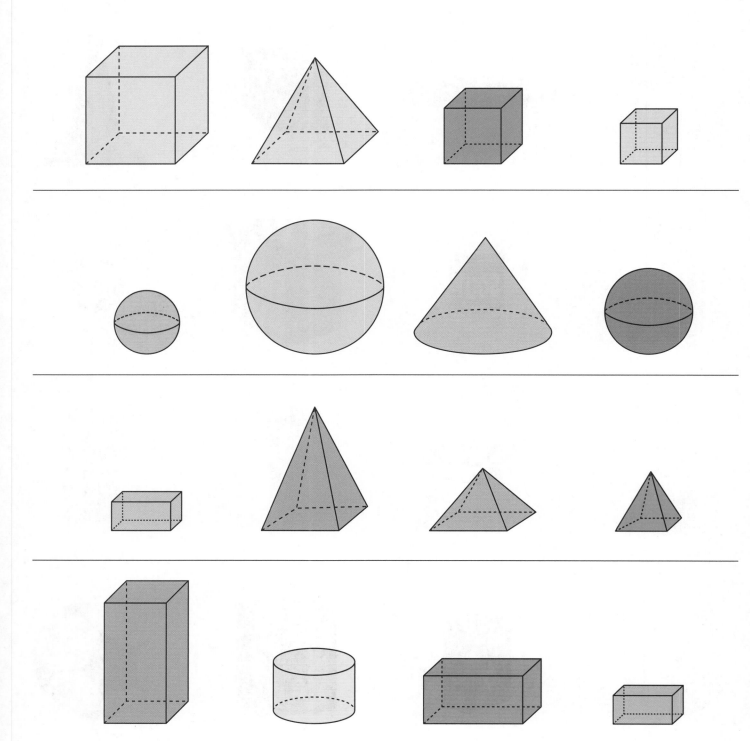

Shape Up

In a three-dimensional shape, a **vertex** is where three or more edges meet. An **edge** is where two sides meet. A **face** is the shape formed by the edges.

WRITE the number of vertices, edges, and faces for each shape.

	Number of Vertices	Number of Edges	Number of Faces

About Face

CIRCLE all of the shapes that are faces on the three-dimensional shape.

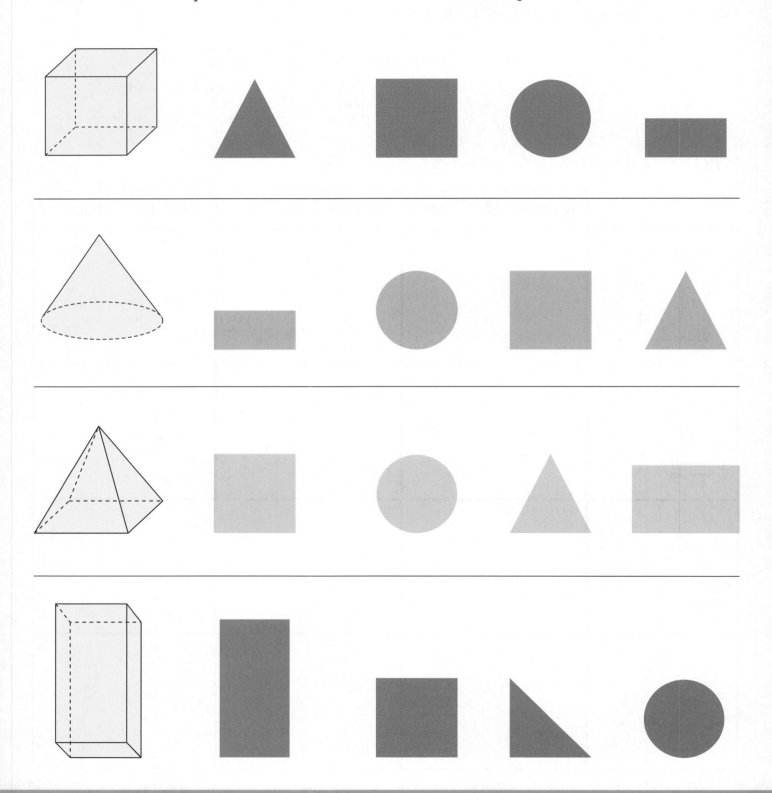

Mirror, Mirror

DRAW a line of symmetry through each picture.

HINT: Some shapes have more than one line of symmetry.

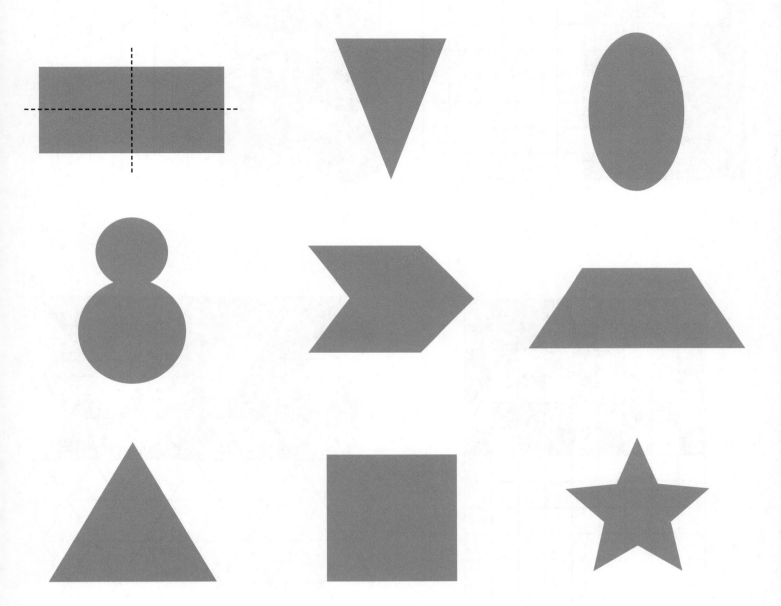

Color Flip

COLOR the pictures so they are symmetrical.

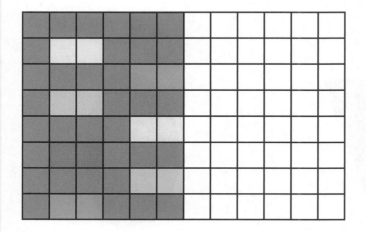

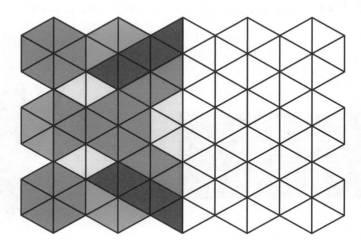

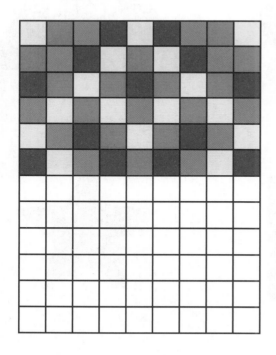

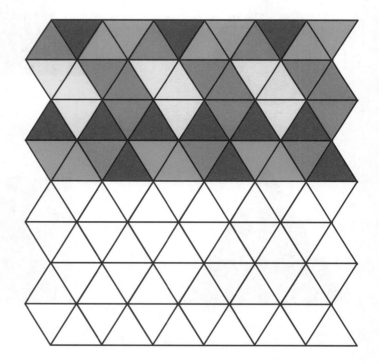

Any Which Way

A **flip**, **slide**, or **turn** has been applied to each shape. WRITE *flip*, *slide*, or *turn* for each pair of shapes.

Example:

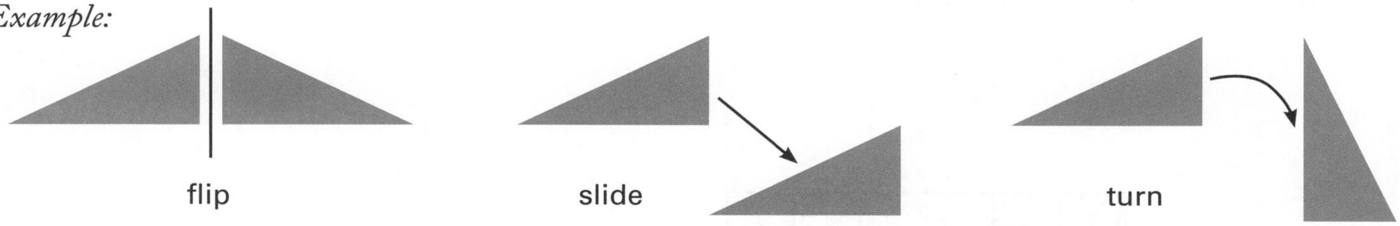

flip   slide   turn

1

2

3

4

5

6

7

8

Perfect Patterns

A **tessellation** is a repeating pattern of shapes that has no gaps or overlapping shapes. DRAW and COLOR the rest of each tessellation.

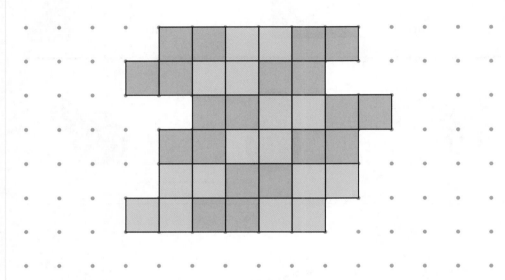

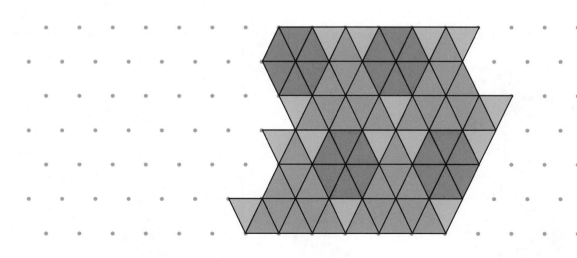

Match Up

DRAW a line to match each shape to its description.

8 sides
8 vertices

5 sides
5 vertices

6 sides
6 vertices

8 edges
5 vertices
5 faces

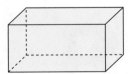

6 edges
4 vertices
4 faces

12 edges
8 vertices
6 faces

Unit Rewind

WRITE the perimeter and area of this rectangle.

1.

6 cm

10 cm

Perimeter: _____ cm

Area: _____ sq cm

DRAW the line or lines of symmetry through each letter.

2.  A

3. D

4. X

WRITE *flip*, *slide*, or *turn*.

Q Q

Z N

R Я

_____ 5

_____ 6

_____ 7

It's about Time

WRITE the time on each clock.

Example:

<u>5</u> : <u>37</u>

1. _____ : _____

2. _____ : _____

3. _____ : _____

4. _____ : _____

5. _____ : _____

6. _____ : _____

Telling Time

Watch It!

DRAW a line to connect each watch to a clock that shows the same time.

Set Your Clock

Each clock has the wrong time. DRAW hands to show the correct time on each clock.

HINT: Add time to a clock that is slow, and subtract time from a clock that is fast.

1.  1 hour and 41 minutes slow ⟶

2.  2 hours and 27 minutes slow ⟶

3.  1 hour and 16 minutes fast ⟶

4.  3 hours and 45 minutes fast ⟶

Time Difference

WRITE the difference in time between each pair of clocks.

1.

1:17   5:58

_____ hours _____ minutes

2.

10:43   12:47

_____ hours _____ minutes

3.

6:36   9:09

_____ hours _____ minutes

4.

7:24   11:11

_____ hours _____ minutes

Tick Tock, Tick Tock

Jake follows the same schedule every day. How much time does he spend doing each activity in five days?

HINT: Multiply each time by 5.

ONE DAY

Eating	1 hour
Watching TV	1 hour 30 minutes
Going to school	6 hours 45 minutes
Reading	45 minutes
Playing soccer	2 hours 15 minutes
Sleeping	8 hours 20 minutes

FIVE DAYS

1. Eating _____ hours _____ minutes

2. Watching TV _____ hours _____ minutes

3. Going to school _____ hours _____ minutes

4. Reading _____ hours _____ minutes

5. Playing soccer _____ hours _____ minutes

6. Sleeping _____ hours _____ minutes

Mad Dash

WRITE how long it took for each person to run one mile. CIRCLE the person who had the fastest time per mile.

HINT: Divide the total time by the number of miles.

 5 miles: 45 minutes

 2 miles: 20 minutes

 8 miles: 64 minutes

 3 miles: 18 minutes

 10 miles: 1 hour 10 minutes

 7 miles: 56 minutes

1. 1 mile: _____ minutes

2. 1 mile: _____ minutes

3. 1 mile: _____ minutes

4. 1 mile: _____ minutes

5. 1 mile: _____ minutes

6. 1 mile: _____ minutes

Cash Crunch

WRITE the total cost to buy all four items.

HINT: Use the money to help you add.

$48

$63.50

$75

$12.25

Total cost _____

Making Change

Using the money to buy each item, how much change will you get back? WRITE the answer for each item.

1. 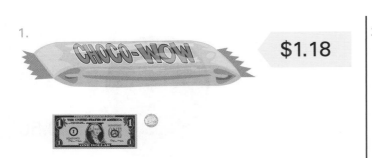 $1.18

Change: _____

2.  $4.45

Change: _____

3.  $28.30

Change: _____

4. 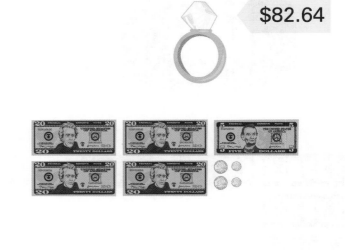 $82.64

Change: _____

Filling Orders

WRITE the total cost of each order.

	GUEST CHECK				
Date	Table	Guests	Server		000903
4	Galaxy Burgers				
2	Sunburst Salads				
1	Freaky Fries				
3	Milky Way Milkshakes				
				Total	

	GUEST CHECK				
Date	Table	Guests	Server		000904
3	Pluto Burgers				
5	Black Hole Burgers				
2	Milky Way Milkshakes				
4	Mars Waters				
				Total	

	GUEST CHECK				
Date	Table	Guests	Server		000905
4	Galaxy Burgers				
9	Pluto Burgers				
3	Sunburst Salads				
6	Freaky Fries				
5	Mars Waters				
				Total	

	GUEST CHECK				
Date	Table	Guests	Server		000906
2	Pluto Burgers				
8	Black Hole Burgers				
2	Sunburst Salads				
5	Freaky Fries				
4	Milky Way Milkshakes				
				Total	

Multiplying & Dividing Money

Best Price

WRITE the cost of one marble. CIRCLE the bag that has the lowest price for one marble.

1.

$36.00

1 marble: _____

2.

$4.50

1 marble: _____

3.

$9.00

1 marble: _____

4.

$20.00

1 marble: _____

5.

$20.00

1 marble: _____

6.

$14.00

1 marble: _____

7.

$12.75

1 marble: _____

8.

$24.00

1 marble: _____

Work It Out

WRITE the answers.

Rita spent 42 minutes riding her bike into town, 28 minutes at the comic book store, 11 minutes at the ice cream shop with her friends, and 54 minutes on the bike ride home.

1. How long was Rita gone? _____ hours _____ minutes

2. If Rita left the house at 3:00, what time did she return home? _____:_____

John goes to the hardware store and buys a hammer for $17.00, 3 screwdrivers for $9.00 each, and 10 screws for 10 cents a piece.

3. How much money does John spend? _____

Joelle makes her own necklaces. Each necklace takes 15 minutes to make and costs her $8.00 in supplies.

4. How long does it take to make 12 necklaces? _____

5. How much would Joelle spend to make 7 necklaces? _____

Unit Rewind

WRITE the time on each clock. Then WRITE the difference in time between them.

1. _____ : _____   _____ : _____   _____ hours _____ minutes

2. _____ : _____   _____ : _____   _____ hours _____ minutes

3. CIRCLE the box with the best price for one donut.

 $12.00    $15.00    $24.00

4. How much would eight robots cost?

$8.00

_____

5. How much would five packs of gum cost?

50¢

_____

Answers

Page 125
1. 5, 0, 8, 1   2. 6, 3, 3, 7
3. 0, 4, 2, 8   4. 9, 9, 6, 3
5. 2, 0, 0, 6   6. 3, 7, 1, 2

Page 126
1. six thousand, four hundred five
2. one thousand, five hundred thirty-eight
3. two thousand, seven hundred eighty
4. four thousand, nine hundred ninety-nine
5. seven thousand, two hundred sixty-three
6. nine thousand, three hundred fourteen
7. 3,576   8. 8,633
9. 5,210   10. 9,891
11. 7,345   12. 1,452

Page 127
1. 3,345   2. 8,229   3. 5,674
4. 1,963   5. 4,516   6. 6,437

Page 128
1. 7,481   2. 2,356   3. 6,292
4. 4,623   5. 9,108   6. 5,534

Page 129
1. <   2. >   3. >
4. <   5. <   6. >
7. >   8. <   9. <
10. >   11. <   12. >
13. >   14. <   15. <

Pages 130
1. >   2. <   3. =
4. >   5. =   6. <

Pages 131
1. 6,672   2. 9,158   3. 5,803
4. 4,910   5. 7,398   6. 3,848

Page 132
1. 4,763   2. 7,848   3. 3,399
4. 6,332   5. 2,165   6. 9,528

Page 133
1. 20   2. 90   3. 40
4. 90   5. 50   6. 80
7. 20   8. 40   9. 500
10. 400   11. 100   12. 800
13. 500   14. 800   15. 600
16. 300

Page 134
1. 7,000   2. 1,000   3. 6,000
4. 8,000   5. 3,000   6. 6,000
7. 9,000   8. 3,000   9. 2,000
10. 4,000   11. 8,000   12. 6,000
13. 4,000   14. 3,000   15. 7,000
16. 4,000

Page 135
Check:
1. $16   2. $240   3. $3,200

Page 136
Check: 167

Page 137
1. 8,421   2. 3,954
3. 5,736   4. 7,677
5. four thousand, three hundred eighty-five

Page 137 (continued)
6. six thousand, five hundred nine
7. seven thousand, one hundred thirty-eight
8. nine thousand, eight hundred seventy
9. 8,421   10. 4,385
11. 3,954   12. 5,736
13. 4,385   14. 9,870

Page 138
1. 8,810   2. 5,187
3. 700   4. 900
5. 900   6. 200
7. 6,000   8. 1,000
9. 7,000   10. 3,000
11. Check: 26

Page 139
1. 83   2. 58   3. 99
4. 67   5. 87   6. 49
7. 93   8. 66   9. 59
10. 48   11. 76   12. 97

Page 140
1. 55   2. 41   3. 10
4. 21   5. 47   6. 15
7. 32   8. 53   9. 31
10. 26   11. 68   12. 12

Page 141
1. 589   2. 894   3. 558
4. 467   5. 977   6. 742

Page 142
1. 447   2. 179   3. 356
4. 895   5. 699   6. 552
7. 748   8. 969   9. 773
10. 496   11. 949   12. 297
13. 664   14. 585   15. 794
16. 476

Page 143
1.
$$\begin{array}{r} 516 \\ + 349 \\ \hline \end{array}$$
500 + 300 = 800
10 + 40 = 50
6 + 9 = + 15
865

2.
$$\begin{array}{r} 399 \\ + 174 \\ \hline \end{array}$$
300 + 100 = 400
90 + 70 = 160
9 + 4 = + 13
573

3.
$$\begin{array}{r} 472 \\ + 225 \\ \hline \end{array}$$
400 + 200 = 600
70 + 20 = 90
2 + 5 = + 7
697

4.
$$\begin{array}{r} 534 \\ + 177 \\ \hline \end{array}$$
500 + 100 = 600
30 + 70 = 100
4 + 7 = + 11
711

5.
$$\begin{array}{r} 290 \\ + 636 \\ \hline \end{array}$$
200 + 600 = 800
90 + 30 = 120
0 + 6 = + 6
926

Page 143 (continued)
6.
$$\begin{array}{r} 198 \\ + 184 \\ \hline \end{array}$$
100 + 100 = 200
90 + 80 = 170
8 + 4 = + 12
382

7.
$$\begin{array}{r} 427 \\ + 296 \\ \hline \end{array}$$
400 + 200 = 600
20 + 90 = 110
7 + 6 = + 13
723

8.
$$\begin{array}{r} 688 \\ + 263 \\ \hline \end{array}$$
600 + 200 = 800
80 + 60 = 140
8 + 3 = + 11
951

Page 144
1. 911   2. 645   3. 791
4. 783   5. 421   6. 505
7. 832   8. 512   9. 932
10. 820   11. 700   12. 657

Page 145
1. 152   2. 423   3. 305
4. 121   5. 211   6. 446

Page 146
1. 714   2. 352   3. 824
4. 513   5. 261   6. 562
7. 442   8. 104   9. 137
10. 318   11. 331   12. 521
13. 705   14. 374   15. 429
16. 680

Page 147
1. 184   2. 208   3. 364
4. 148   5. 59   6. 289

Page 148
1. 288   2. 452   3. 696
4. 117   5. 228   6. 176
7. 245   8. 87   9. 689
10. 55   11. 148   12. 325

Page 149
1. 283   2. 175   3. 443
4. 246   5. 185   6. 19
7. 569   8. 657   9. 335
10. 149   11. 298   12. 72

Page 150
1. 350   2. 468   3. 279
4. 176   5. 356   6. 123
7. 286   8. 98   9. 293
10. 437   11. 89   12. 269
13. 122   14. 687   15. 162
16. 361

Page 151
1. 20   2. 17   3. 25
4. 50   5. 69   6. 185
7. 136   8. 143   9. 249
10. 513   11. 721   12. 800
13. 170   14. 226   15. 718
16. 959

Page 152
1. 161   2. 519   3. 790
4. 964   5. 152   6. 773
7. 625   8. 870

Page 153
1. 5,286   2. 3,737   3. 9,383
4. 7,820   5. 6,659   6. 4,745
7. 1,815   8. 4,006   9. 2,897
10. 7,589   11. 5,553   12. 6,738
13. 6,221   14. 3,426   15. 4,113
16. 9,805

Page 154
1. 6,511   2. 1,326   3. 4,484
4. 5,073   5. 9,262   6. 7,314
7. 4,939   8. 1,992   9. 1,121
10. 5,470   11. 3,442   12. 4,117
13. 3,478   14. 2,779   15. 7,454
16. 2,909

Page 155
1.
$$\begin{array}{r} 423 \\ + 271 \\ \hline 694 \end{array} \qquad \begin{array}{r} 400 \\ + 200 \\ \hline 600 \end{array}$$

2.
$$\begin{array}{r} 190 \\ + 724 \\ \hline 914 \end{array} \qquad \begin{array}{r} 100 \\ + 700 \\ \hline 800 \end{array}$$

3.
$$\begin{array}{r} 2,385 \\ + 612 \\ \hline 2,997 \end{array} \qquad \begin{array}{r} 2,000 \\ + 600 \\ \hline 2,600 \end{array}$$

4.
$$\begin{array}{r} 8,732 \\ + 958 \\ \hline 9,690 \end{array} \qquad \begin{array}{r} 8,000 \\ + 900 \\ \hline 8,900 \end{array}$$

5.
$$\begin{array}{r} 3,361 \\ + 4,518 \\ \hline 7,879 \end{array} \qquad \begin{array}{r} 3,000 \\ + 4,000 \\ \hline 7,000 \end{array}$$

6.
$$\begin{array}{r} 2,112 \\ + 1,308 \\ \hline 3,420 \end{array} \qquad \begin{array}{r} 2,000 \\ + 1,000 \\ \hline 3,000 \end{array}$$

Page 156
1.
$$\begin{array}{r} 872 \\ - 661 \\ \hline 211 \end{array} \qquad \begin{array}{r} 800 \\ - 600 \\ \hline 200 \end{array}$$

2.
$$\begin{array}{r} 925 \\ - 629 \\ \hline 296 \end{array} \qquad \begin{array}{r} 900 \\ - 600 \\ \hline 300 \end{array}$$

3.
$$\begin{array}{r} 6,734 \\ - 322 \\ \hline 6,412 \end{array} \qquad \begin{array}{r} 6,000 \\ - 300 \\ \hline 5,700 \end{array}$$

4.
$$\begin{array}{r} 1,283 \\ - 564 \\ \hline 719 \end{array} \qquad \begin{array}{r} 1,000 \\ - 500 \\ \hline 500 \end{array}$$

5.
$$\begin{array}{r} 4,826 \\ - 1,711 \\ \hline 3,115 \end{array} \qquad \begin{array}{r} 4,000 \\ - 1,000 \\ \hline 3,000 \end{array}$$

6.
$$\begin{array}{r} 9,382 \\ - 7,449 \\ \hline 1,933 \end{array} \qquad \begin{array}{r} 9,000 \\ - 7,000 \\ \hline 2,000 \end{array}$$

Answers

Page 157

1. 436   400
    + 251 + 300
    ——— ———
    687   700

2. 166   200
    + 108 + 100
    ——— ———
    274   300

3. 3,524 3,500
    + 367 + 400
    ——— ———
    3,891 3,900

4. 7,539 7,500
    + 616 + 600
    ——— ———
    8,155 8,100

5. 2,345 2,300
    + 2,354 + 2,400
    ——— ———
    4,699 4,700

6. 4,181 4,200
    + 1,423 + 1,400
    ——— ———
    5,604 5,600

Page 158

1. 878   900
    − 223 − 200
    ——— ———
    655   700

2. 795   800
    − 519 − 500
    ——— ———
    276   300

3. 6,428 6,400
    − 411 − 400
    ——— ———
    6,017 6,000

4. 4,493 4,500
    − 897 − 900
    ——— ———
    3,596 3,600

5. 8,781 8,800
    − 6,447 − 6,400
    ——— ———
    2,334 2,400

6. 7,064 7,100
    − 1,815 − 1,800
    ——— ———
    5,249 5,300

Page 159
1. 548 2. 8,804 3. 107

Page 160
1. 349 2. 623 3. 297

Page 161
1. 75   2. 111   3. 22
4. 39   5. 678   6. 931
7. 305   8. 294   9. 1,794
10. 5,600 11. 3,061 12. 6,609
13. 8,959 14. 7,012 15. 631
16. 1,327

Page 162

1. 531   500   500
    + 324 + 300 + 300
    ——— ——— ———
    855   800   800

2. 1,249 1,000 1,200
    + 217 + 200 + 200
    ——— ——— ———
    1,466 1,200 1,400

3. 352   300   400
    − 144 − 100 − 100
    ——— ——— ———
    208   200   300

4. 4,671 4,000 4,700
    − 728 − 700 − 700
    ——— ——— ———
    3,943 3,300 4,000

Page 163
1. 4   2. 12
3. 24   4. 16

Page 164
1. 10   2. 8
3. 5   4. 4

Page 165

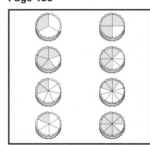

Page 166
1. 8   2. 12   3. 4
4. 14   5. 6

Page 167
1. 15   2. 27   3. 21
4. 24   5. 40

Page 168
1. 20   2. 5   3. 35
4. 30   5. 10   6. 45
7. 25   8. 40   9. 50
10. 15

Page 169
1. 6   2. 0   3. 3
4. 0   5. 10 6. 0
7. 5   8. 0   9. 1
10. 0 11. 9 12. 0
13. 7 14. 0 15. 8
16. 0 17. 2 18. 0

Page 170
1. 28 2. 30 3. 48
4. 36 5. 60

Page 171
1. 10 2. 32 3. 100
4. 27 5. 35 6. 6
7. 30 8. 0   9. 12
10. 49 11. 54 12. 25
13. 16 14. 36 15. 21
16. 0 17. 64 18. 2

Page 172
1. 4   2. 35 3. 24
4. 12 5. 45 6. 20
7. 36 8. 0   9. 8
10. 81 11. 28 12. 15
13. 80 14. 0 15. 36
16. 30 17. 16 18. 16
19. 21 20. 72 21. 8
22. 1 23. 18 24. 45
25. 20 26. 40 27. 0
28. 18 29. 50 30. 9

Page 173
1. 6   2. 10 3. 4

Page 174
1. 6   2. 4
3. 2   4. 8

Page 175
1. 3   2. 5
3. 9   4. 6

Page 176
1. 6   2. 4   3. 5
4. 9   5. 2

Page 177
1. 8   2. 3   3. 10
4. 7   5. 7   6. 2
7. 7   8. 8   9. 8
10. 6 11. 9 12. 6
13. 9 14. 3 15. 7
16. 3 17. 4 18. 10

Page 178
1. 4   2. 10 3. 2
4. 9   5. 8   6. 5
7. 9   8. 7   9. 6
10. 9 11. 4 12. 3
13. 3 14. 5 15. 4
16. 6 17. 8 18. 8
19. 3 20. 10 21. 9
22. 7 23. 9 24. 7
25. 9 26. 2 27. 10
28. 5 29. 8 30. 4

Page 179
1. 1, 2, 4
2. 1, 2, 3, 6
3. 1, 3, 9
4. 1, 2, 3, 4, 6, 12
5. 1, 3, 5, 15
6. 1, 2, 4, 8, 16
7. 1, 2, 3, 6, 9, 18

Page 180

	2				10	
12	10	16	35	20	40
4	8	6	70	36	72
3	15	20	50	80	30

	6				8	
40	14	12	56	36	24
25	54	36	27	80	64
35	8	18	48	34	30

Page 181
1. 50, 40, 15, 20
2. 18

Page 182
1. 6, 2   2. 8

Page 183
1. 15 2. 72 3. 24
4. 5   5. 0   6. 20
7. 64 8. 9   9. 45
10. 16 11. 63 12. 28
13. 36 14. 60 15. 0
16. 48 17. 81 18. 18
19. 4 20. 6 21. 5
22. 7 23. 1 24. 2
25. 9 26. 7 27. 10
28. 3 29. 6 30. 3
31. 5 32. 2 33. 4
34. 8 35. 3 36. 7

Page 184
1. 5 × 2 = 10   2. 6 × 3 = 18
    2 × 5 = 10   3 × 6 = 18
    10 ÷ 5 = 2   18 ÷ 6 = 3
    10 ÷ 2 = 5   18 ÷ 3 = 6

3. 4 × 7 = 28   4. 3 × 10 = 30
    7 × 4 = 28   10 × 3 = 30
    28 ÷ 4 = 7   30 ÷ 3 = 10
    28 ÷ 7 = 4   30 ÷ 10 = 3

Page 185
1. $\frac{1}{2}$ 2. $\frac{3}{4}$ 3. $\frac{2}{3}$

4. $\frac{2}{5}$ 5. $\frac{3}{8}$ 6. $\frac{5}{6}$

Page 186

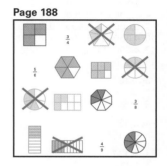

Page 187
1. $\frac{2}{3}$ 2. $\frac{5}{6}$ 3. $\frac{1}{4}$

4. $\frac{4}{7}$ 5. $\frac{6}{8}$ 6. $\frac{1}{10}$

7. $\frac{6}{9}$ 8. $\frac{3}{5}$

Page 188

Answers

Page 189

1. $\dfrac{4}{8}$ 2. $\dfrac{1}{5}$ 3. $\dfrac{7}{9}$

4. $\dfrac{2}{6}$ 5. $\dfrac{6}{10}$ 6. $\dfrac{3}{7}$

Page 190

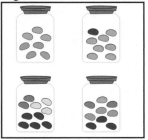

Page 191

1. $\dfrac{3}{7}$ 2. $\dfrac{5}{7}$ 3. $\dfrac{2}{3}$

4. $\dfrac{2}{4}$ 5. $\dfrac{1}{3}$ 6. $\dfrac{3}{4}$

Page 192

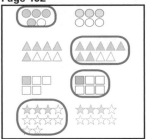

Page 193

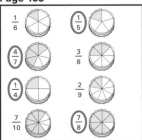

Page 194

1. >   2. >   3. <
4. =   5. <   6. >
7. <   8. <   9. >
10. >   11. >   12. =

Page 195

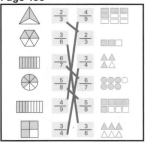

Page 196

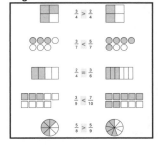

Page 197

1. 2, 5   2. 5, 13
3. 3, 8   4. 4, 10

Page 198

1. 3, 8   2. 1, 3   3. 5, 13
4. 2, 5   5. 4, 11   6. 6, 15

Page 199

1. inch   2. inch   3. foot
4. foot   5. yard

Page 200

1. centimeter
2. meter
3. centimeter
4. meter
5. meter
6. centimeter

Page 201

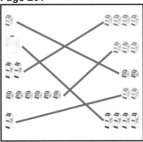

Page 202

1. gallon   2. cup
3. pint   4. gallon
5. cup   6. quart
7. gallon   8. pint

Page 203

Page 204

1. milliliter   2. liter
3. milliliter   4. milliliter
5. liter   6. milliliter
7. liter   8. liter

Page 205

Page 206

1. ounce   2. pound
3. ounce   4. pound
5. pound   6. ounce
7. ounce   8. pound

Page 207

Page 208

1. gram   2. kilogram
3. gram   4. gram
5. kilogram   6. gram
7. gram   8. kilogram

Page 209

1. 68, 20   2. 41, 5
3. 50, 10   4. 95, 35
5. 32, 0   6. 77, 25

Page 210

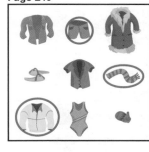

Page 211

1. 4, 10   2. 2, 5
3. 3, 8   4. 6, 15

Page 212

1. pound   2. gallon
3. gram   4. yard
5. quart   6. gallon
7. milliliter   8. meter

Page 213

1. <   2. >   3. =
4. >   5. =   6. <
7. >   8. <   9. >
10. =   11. <   12. >

Page 214

1. meter   2. degrees
3. gram   4. cup
5. pound   6. centimeter
7. gallon   8. inch

Page 215

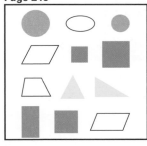

Page 216

	Number of vertices	Number of sides
	3	3
	4	4
	3	3
	6	6
	4	4

Answers

Page 217
1. 23
2. 22
3. 40
4. 27

Page 218
1. 15
2. 16
3. 12
4. 30
5. 54
6. 25

Page 219

Page 220

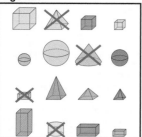

Page 221

	Number of vertices	Number of edges	Number of faces
	8	12	6
	5	8	5
	8	12	6
	4	6	4

Page 222

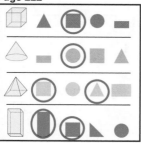

Page 223

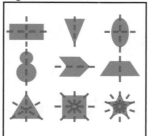

Page 224

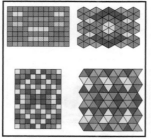

Page 225
1. fllp
2. turn
3. slide
4. flip
5. turn
6. slide
7. flip
8. turn

Page 226

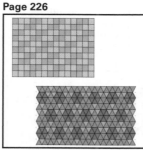

Page 227

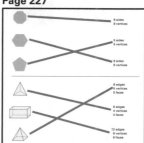

8 sides
8 vertices

5 sides
5 vertices

6 sides
6 vertices

8 edges
5 vertices
5 faces

6 edges
4 vertices
4 faces

12 edges
8 vertices
6 faces

Page 228
1. 32, 60
2. **A**
3. **D**
4. **X**
5. slide
6. turn
7. flip

Page 229
1. 10:02
2. 6:18
3. 2:44
4. 9:51
5. 11:27
6. 3:33

Page 230

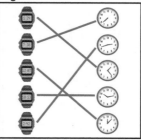

Page 231

Page 232
1. 4, 41
2. 2, 4
3. 2, 33
4. 3, 47

Page 233
1. 5, 0
2. 7, 30
3. 33, 45
4. 3, 45
5. 11, 15
6. 41, 40

Page 234
1. 9
2. 10
3. 8
4. 6
5. 7
6. 8

Fastest time per mile:

Page 235
$ 198.75

Page 236
1. $ 0.07
2. $ 1.05
3. $ 1.70
4. $ 3.06

Page 237

GUEST CHECK   000903

4	Galaxy Burgers	$20.00
2	Sunburst Salads	$20.00
1	Freaky Fries	$2.00
3	Milky Way Milkshakes	$9.00
	Total	$51.00

GUEST CHECK   000904

3	Pluto Burgers	$21.00
5	Black Hole Burgers	$45.00
2	Milky Way Milkshakes	$6.00
4	Mars Waters	$4.00
	Total	$76.00

Page 237 (continued)

GUEST CHECK   000905

4	Galaxy Burgers	$20.00
9	Pluto Burgers	$63.00
3	Sunburst Salads	$30.00
6	Freaky Fries	$12.00
5	Mars Waters	$5.00
	Total	$130.00

GUEST CHECK   000906

2	Pluto Burgers	$14.00
8	Black Hole Burgers	$72.00
2	Sunburst Salads	$20.00
5	Freaky Fries	$10.00
4	Milky Way Milkshakes	$12.00
	Total	$128.00

Page 238
1. $6.00
2. $2.25
3. $1.00
4. $5.00
5. $2.00
6. $2.00
7. $4.25
8. $3.00

Lowest price for 1 marble:

Page 239
1. 2, 15
2. 5:15
3. $45.00
4. 3 hours
5. $56.00

Page 240
1. 9:17, 12:51, 3, 34
2. 11:34, 4:43, 5, 9
3. Donuts $12.00
4. $64.00
5. $2.50

Sylvan for Every Student!

SINGLE-SUBJECT WORKBOOKS

☑ Focus on individual skills and subjects

☑ Fun activities and grade-appropriate exercises

3-IN-1 SUPER WORKBOOKS

☑ Three Sylvan single-subject workbooks in one package for just $18.99!

☑ Perfect practice for the student who needs to focus on a range of topics

FUN ON THE RUN ACTIVITY BOOKS

☑ Just $3.99/$4.75 Can.

☑ Colorful games and activities for on-the-go learning

FLASHCARD SETS

☑ Spelling and vocabulary for Pre-K–5th grade

☑ Math for Pre-K–5th grade

PAGE PER DAY WORKBOOKS

☑ Perforated pages—perfect for your child to do just one workbook page each day

☑ Extra practice the easy way!

KICK START PACKAGES

☑ Includes books, flashcards, access to online activities, and more

☑ Everything your child needs in one comprehensive package

Try FREE pages today at SylvanPagePerDay.com

1000

Moms, Dads, Teachers, and Homeschoolers Give Rave Reviews!

"**Samantha loves these books** because to her, they are not schoolwork. They are fun activities. But really she is learning, and doing the same work she does at school."

—MommyMandy.com

"As an early childhood teacher, I know that good reading, vocabulary, and spelling skills make an essential foundation for both academic success as well as lifelong learning. **Sylvan Learning Workbooks & Learning Kits** are an awesome resource that I'd have no problem recommending to the parents of any of my students who are struggling."

—TheOpinionatedParent.com

"As a teacher, I look for different aspects in a resource than a student or a parent might. . . . **The book has vibrant, attractive colors, and the worksheets are really fun.** My 10-year-old son has been enjoying them since I got the book. . . . I recommend this book to students, parents, and teachers alike for increasing student achievement."

—DynamiteLessonPlan.com

"If you are looking for some **good, fun learning books for your child,** I definitely recommend the Sylvan Learning series."

—TheDadJam.com